The Dar

UNIVERSITY OF WESTERN AUSTRALIA PRESS NEW WRITING SERIES

In 2005, its seventieth year of publishing academic and general titles, UWA Press launched a *New Writing* series, with a focus on creative writing. We commenced the series by sourcing novels and shorter prose works from postgraduate writing programs in universities across Australia, which for the last three decades have produced exciting new works from emerging and established writers. By introducing the series in this way we recognised the role of Australian universities in nurturing and supporting writers, and contributing to the continuing production of Australian writing. Since our launch of the series we have included other works: short story collections, poetry, and literary non-fiction, and reached out more broadly than Australia to include a range of exciting writers.

Series editor Terri-ann White is actively involved in the literary culture of Australia: as a writer, bookseller, editor, award judge, and publisher. Her novel *Finding Theodore and Brina* (2001) is studied in university courses in Spain, the United States and Australia. She published a collection of stories, *Night and Day*, in 1994, has edited anthologies and been published widely. She is currently director of UWA Press and of a cross-disciplinary research centre at The University of Western Australia.

TITLES IN SERIES

A New Map of the Universe, ANNABEL SMITH
Cusp, JOSEPHINE WILSON
The Concerto Inn, JO GARDINER
The Seamstress, GERALDINE WOOLLER
Paydirt, KATHLEEN MARY FALLON
The Mystery of the Cleaning Lady, SUE WOOLFE
The Last Book You Read, EWAN MORRISON
A History of the Beanbag, SUSAN MIDALIA
The Poet Who Forgot, CATHERINE COLE
Wild Bees: New and Selected Poems, MARTIN HARRISON
The Darwin Poems, EMILY BALLOU

FORTHCOMING

Why She Loves Him, WENDY JAMES

The Darwin Poems

EMILY BALLOU

University of Western Australia Press

First published in 2009 by
University of Western Australia Press
Crawley, Western Australia 6009
www.uwapress.uwa.edu.au

This project has been assisted by the Australian Government through
the Australia Council, its arts funding and advisory body.

Australian Government

Copyright © Emily Ballou 2009

The moral right of the author has been asserted.

The following poems have previously been published:

'Handel, January 17, 1836'
'Falls at Weatherboard, January 17, 1836'
'Blue Vapour, January 17, 1836': Brooks, D. and McMahon, E. (eds),
Southerly Vol. 66 No. 2, 2006.

'Emma': Indyk, I. (ed.), *Heat 14: New Series.*

'Lesson': *Australian Literary Review (ALR)*

'Darwin's Noah'
'On the Subject of Untimely Extinction': *New Madrid, A Journal of Contemporary
Literature, Winter 2009, Intelligent Design Issue.*

'August 3, 1868' was shortlisted in the Virginia Warbey Poetry Prize 2008.

National Library of Australia
Cataloguing-in-Publication entry:

Ballou, Emily.
The Darwin poems / Emily Ballou.
1st ed.
978 1 921401 27 5 (pbk.)
New writing
Bibliography.
Darwin, Charles, 1809–1882 —Poetry.
A821.4

Cover Image: Portrait of Charles Darwin, Down House, English Heritage Images

Typeset in 10pt Janson by Lasertype
Printed by Griffin Press

To Ewan,
with love

"*Poetry is not
the proper antithesis
to prose
but to science.
Poetry is opposed to science.*"

DEFINITION OF POETRY
– SAMUEL TAYLOR COLERIDGE

CONTENTS

– III –

– IV –

– V –

– VI –

– VII –

– I –

"*I seem to remember him gently touching any flower he delighted in… It ran through all his relations to natural things—a most keen feeling of their aliveness.*"

– FRANCIS DARWIN

The Donkey, August, 1817

All along the roads the beds of grass played dead
that summer, the long blades bending under the weight of rain.

Charles walked forever, legs unbound by fence or distance
a silver net of droplets over his hair.
He wandered the river
casting plonking skipping stones
pulling worms to hook
his nails thin black crescents.

The air, the quivering air
carried him, its damp brew of scent
that rose from the ground
that fell from the trees
honeysuckle, dirt, cow dung, field grass, wildflower, hay, leaf
he trod under foot.

He gulped down deep breaths as his father, the Doctor, did
trying to swallow the words for what he felt.
Beneath the pine trees the insects lived & prayed.
Still he killed them.

His pockets belched
treasure to hoard back praise:
black beetle carapaces, crumbling butterfly wings, pads of moss,
quartz-cored rocks
he smashed open on fence posts

spooking the grey, sag-bellied, sad-eyed donkey
who believed he was a sheep among sheep
dumbly tearing grass
heeeeee!
taking off across the field.

Some of the Irish servants believed
donkeys genuflected on Christmas Day
but this one couldn't protect the flock from foxes
& every week in Spring a new dead sheep—
a ram with a hole in its forehead
stigmata from another ram's horns—
lay petrified on its side
bloated, fly-blown, fur black-clotted with mud
until the farmer dragged it away.

His mother's body too
had grown toxic.
Sprouted a fatal mushroom
like a field after rain
& all the world that had seemed
to be made of glass
ecstatic, transparent, mysteriously molten
had broken.

No amount of plunder
no collected cache of wonders could extract
the adoration he now needed

to chase away the terrible secret
growing daily within him:
the thought
that either his father was no doctor
or God was a donkey.

The Plums

in the bowl
on the round table
by the windows
were laid out for
his father.

That pyramid of dark plums
in the shallow Wedgwood bowl—
nearly black when ripe
ruby-lipped when not
oily, reflective, satin-skinned
piled on a plate in the sun—
infinitely pinchable, infinitely delicate, hot
when Charles touched them
when he inserted the tip of his smallest finger
into their dark navels
from which stems had long fallen.

If his father waited too long
to eat them, the plums
would wrinkle & weep
rubbed under thumbs.

At first Charles would pocket a few
pile them in the stores cupboard
or under the piano lid
& reap the glory when he found them
again, his father's missing fruit.

Then he began to flinch a bite of one, two
searching out the perfect plum.
He pulled the skin off them with his teeth
watched beads of blood pinprick the surface
ripped bits of peeling
around the pink sponge.
Old plums were soft & purple, not crisp.
New plums sour & crunched
too much, hard yellow pulp
inedible. He left them all
ruined by the river
the single bite he'd taken from each
like a torn smile.

June, 1828

"My dear Fox, I am dying
 by inches
 from not having anybody
 to talk to
 about insects."

Sappho

Sappho, the Pointer, trailed him
through the town
kept her eye on the hem
of his gown
as it warped & flowed
like the river Cam
& kept her ear on the leather thwack
of his boot soles
against the cobblestones
of the bridge.

The barges slowed with their heft & waft
of smells, the muck
of water she longed to snuffle
down in the green reeds where dead bird & rat
floated. Bloated. Shouts
of bargemen
their voices so much louder
so much fiercer
than his.

Streets were meat
a ripe raw stink of men.

She liked best days in the fens
when together they snorted
the long grass & he crawled
beside her, rooting at the dirt

revelling in discoveries
he'd show then snatch away again.
Sometimes he leapt
like a lunatic, net in hand.
He tore bark off trees, stripping them back
to the pale blue scent of wood
& clasped his greedy fingers
around the quick black bugs.
Sappho drank from muddy puddles
full of clouds.

He did not lead her home then
but stopped at the ill-lit den
where she waited for hours
scratching & licking the gutters
or huddled in a corner
one eye on the door
until he swayed out
murmuring to her
like warm milk.

She knew the tenor of his talk
& the taste of his happiness
the thunder of sudden anger
& the small whisper of sorrow
that sometimes stalked him.
She turned quickly
trying to catch it, to chase it away
with her bark.

She told it to go.
She told it not to come back.

She knew the brew
of his brain & soon knew
that energetic tickle in the air
near his hands, the hop he gave
when something
wild & marvellous
struck him.

She knew the boredom of books
& the smell of his sleep
at the hour of rats, the click
their claws made down the wet streets
she could smell
the drag of their tails
until noon the next day.

She knew the smell of the bed they shared
through the gates & up
the tired stairs
dog & man
this furred, blurred curl of two.

The Very Last Meeting of The Glutton Club

In his dream
the Glutton Club
met yet again
to dine on strange flesh.

Each time
there was a new offering
'unknown to human palate'
that one member
had shot & brought
to the Cambridge cooks
to prepare.

The soft Brown Owl
the last they had tried
& failed to eat—
whose stringy, gamey breast
clung to its bones in protest
as it boiled in the pot
its stomach still full
of ripped fur, the beak-broken bones of mouse—
still haunted.
Its severed head in the bin, eyes open
watching him.

This time
Charles vowed to try harder.

He saw the bowl
smeared with translucent
fish-egg-like meat
& politely asked its origin.
"Penguin," the Gents answered
handing him a spoon.

In The Old Library

Where John Milton
'The Lady of Christ's' & son of a scrivener once sat
composing his Latin oration:
Sportive Exercises on occasion do not stand in the way
of Philosophical Studies
after recovering from a first year
quarrel with his tutor over his assertive, unusurpable singularity
(which resulted in short suspension, not to mention
a good caning at the hands of the Master)
to become one of the more playful & popular fellows,
creating such cunning prolusions as the above as well as
     breaking out
into heroic couplets instead of the usual formal tongue
& leaving behind among the twine & leather-bound
book & tome-stacked shelves a lasting battle
of light & darkness, 'a little world' not yet spent
so two hundred years later
Charles Darwin, pale & Paleyfied, just twenty-one,
solemnly bent his head & read
his favourite poem.

Venus

He hurried past Elijah and the angel
Christ calling Zacchaeus, past Abraham
journeying to the land of Canaan, and St Jerome
lost in the wilderness, to the place
where the velvet curtains parted.

The guards were quite used to the queue of young men
the hot hum of them, filing through the new rooms.
Leather soles echoed on stone floors
gave their heart beats away.

Entering the dim boudoir
she was waiting there, on the crimson couch
flute in hand, looking at him.

Some troubadour with a lute had trumped him
and was trying to win her with his music.
Confusingly, astonishingly, she was
already bare
but for a cord of pearls, a torn piece
of gauze over her sex.

Even the soft streaks of daylight
had found their way through the folds
of the curtains to catch a look
and had laid down upon the dark-red drapes behind her hair,
a musculature of warm wet silk.

Her cheeks, her breasts, indeed
the rounds of her knees
all pink. Her supple, open
opal skin made him
think of an apple
plucked from a branch, mid-air;
a blood-tinged handful, tart and sweet.

Burn This!—

*"So I suppose I must trust to fate
for a master or wait till you come."*
– Fanny Owen to Charles Darwin

She felt she would rot
with waiting

the stuffed armchairs
never moved an inch no matter
how much she stretched out

or shook them
& she agitated
sometimes furiously

so fate would not
mistake her for a chair
& leave her an eternity
to some ticking despair

by the fire with her novels
until the Governor
ordered her back to the easel & brush
a painted green scene
she could see but not touch.

Through the long windows
the frost closed her in.
Her father, her keeper
gone with the family

the house so quiet she could hear
a tread on the stairs two storeys up
or the sound of four clouds
rushing past to ballrooms
at Brighton town.
Her days' only notable moments
were the seven deliveries of the post
when she hoped one of the packets
held one from him, her dear Charley
eminently shootable young Sir
who sometimes deigned to visit her
in her desolate black Forest—
though lately, more & more rarely.

Once just a morning's canter away
he was now lost to the University
where he stalked to the wood
with manic zeal
for some rare elusive beetle.

"Dear Dr Postillion,
I've been so busy
so cold and *frost bitten*
that I haven't had time
to scribble a few lines.
I'm sure the *dear little beetles*
are keeping you fine.
How, by the way, does the *mania* go?

As for me, yr dutiful Housemaid
I've not been outside the Barriers
of the Fortress in days…"

He'd taught her to shoot
till her shoulder turned blackblue
& the two of them rolled
in the strawberry beds
stretched out like beasts.
They took home empty baskets
stained mouths, inflamed lips.
Her skin itched with him
& with something else
she couldn't quite name,
a new inability
to tame this daily agitation
this rage
ill with waiting, ill-tempered
for her life to begin.

Her words on the white vacant page
just a stupid scrawl
but she would never write *'like a Lady'. Adieu!*
Burn this--as soon as read
or tremble with my revenge.
She cured her fury
galloping on the Downs.
If this was her bliss
so be it.

The problem as she saw it
with a lady in general
was her need to be haltered—
& whether a lady herself found
the *Hare* in question halterable, or shootable, or not—
was not the concern. To manage the shoot
without being shot first was a matter of gamble
a game of écarte. All she could hope for
with the Red Coats and Moustachios
was to be her own Master
of mystery, while she waited all season
to be caught & sent
in the utmost ar mony
to the King's Bench.

But in moments of cold
coop & weakness
she had the dreadful sense
her life would be
one long postponement, confinement
remarkably useless
& not five and twenty
bachelors at a Rigadoon
nor outings in the family Van
could save her.

She could already hear the Duns
beginning to ride.

And as much as she
wanted, from pure
sheer boredom
to be *taken alive*
in heated fancy
she would not wait for him.
Whoever stepped in first
to halter her hand
could have her
could lead her out
of this dark, wooded house
into future, status
& quo.

The Beach

1.

All along the scratched stretches of beach land
when the tide was tugging back, some evenings
the low pools, miniature seas
contained everything
he could imagine, everything he'd ever
want to see, and more. Bounties of being.

In the opal light, the flats left organ-shaped puddles,
sucking quicksand he squelched through.
He liked the deep squelch around his boots, eyes
to the ground, scouring the stony, spongy surface
trying to disappear.

He tried to banish the thought, newly lodged,
that man's consciousness was mere brain, waves
pushing pebbles forward and backwards over the beach.

The grey-blue clouds, milk-topped, spread long and low.
His shadow preceded him, painted proof on the sand
of his existence; the gold engine of sunlight
as inexplicable and shape-shifting as melting glass
streaming behind the humped Edinburgh hills.

The patterning of gulls on the shore
a huddled form
that altered as he edged closer.
Their feet left triangled marks of retreat.

A lone gull, far from the flock, experimented
with the limits of water, pecked at stones.
When he chortled at its waddle, its purpose and poise
it turned its head as if to say:
"What is so very amusing?"
And pattered on, away,
to do some more of what it did so well.

2.

You could squat down for an hour near a tidal pool
and await the tiniest sway of cilia, or a glimpse
of feathery sea-pen, hovering at the edge
to discover a colony of tentacled polyps; or hurl
your chanced find of grey, furred sea mice back
into the sea like stones
and watch them turn into balls, and watch
them roll back up onto the beach with waves
and stand finally, aching, to stretch and let
out a long, deep growl
of pleasure and be struck
by a sudden bolt of light in the eyes
as if you had dissolved back up
into the sun.

3.

The beach just was. *Is.*
It had no idea how it got there.
But to dig back the sand with two hands as he had
as a child, searching its beginning
with his particular gift of persistence
with his willingness to understand what it truly was
while his sisters called: *It never ends. It will never end*
still did not seem to be an impossible task.

4.

That day he had dug until the water
streaming through the sand collapsed his hole and sand
was no longer sand—quite—in this form.
It flowed, liquid, becoming something else across his palms.
He dug another and another hole, each time
trying to find the bottom of the world
before the sea caved in.

Stop! You will exhaust yourself!
his sisters cried.

You cannot hold it, just behold it.

It is what it is. And nothing more.

5.

When the sun becomes a cross of orange light
and puddles darken the shore and stones
become miniature mountains in the glow
and the sand blows—
stop and stretch again, the gulls are flying.

Soon,
the crags of the old town will be
clawed by birds
flown in with fog from the sea
circling the air above steeple and castle
with their distinct ache, their screams.

His sisters said to put his faith
not in this world
but the next.

But look how it shines.

– II –

Tell Nancy to make me 12 shirts
send them up in my carpet bag,
my slippers, a pair of lightest walking shoes.
My Spanish books: my new microscope…
my geological compass…
Have my shirts marked DARWIN.

– CHARLES DARWIN, 1831

Dearest Charley,

"Father thinks
you are wasting
the best years of your life
on ship-board."

Plunge

You thrust your head through a lid of water
open-eyed to the sting of salt
that takes some time to adjust to
then look around.
Your curls swim. Fish scatter.

Pink velvet starfish cling to the green
slopes of sub-aqueous rock pools, the diorama spill
of strange flowers, opening, shutting mouths
draw you deeper
past grey-eyed cuttlefish
the circular gills barely perceptible
feathered edges of constant motion among the waving
fronds of seaweed hair & the rise & pop of silver
domes of air.

Here a corrosive, rusted land
beneath land, a forgotten twin place
on Earth where Man
does not belong, where sea
divides head from body
so thoroughly it is exiled;
the floating flesh
so much whiter, more defenceless;
this total, plunging, breathless despair.

Terror makes you leap up
suddenly from the depths
& laugh to find you were dunked
head down in two feet of water.

Go now. Deeper. Into the blue swallow.
If you're lucky enough you'll catch
a fever of sting rays
soaring past the ship in sinuous series
the great, slate, rugose weights;
little bodies embedded in wings.

When you capture one
& flip over its flat white belly, on the sand,
a small false face appears:
the side-gazing eyes
the nose-holes of its snout, the slit
of mouth gills dimpled on either side
like a smile—
wide, distended, intelligent
underwater humanity
you slice with a knife.

Nights when the sea
& everything you touch
lights up green, pours over you
mass & massive

you will remember
Volta's batteries
which he called his electric fish
& which were puzzled out
from the anatomy
of stingrays.

The Vanishing

Something peculiar happens
when you make that Southern crossing
something besides the *Beagle's* equatorial initiation;
black pitch to the face
skin lathered with tar, shaved by saw, dunked in salt,
plummeting
into the upside down realm, ship adrift.
The line happens. You cross it. Then something
else happens.

Father, you tried to teach me to be frugal, to eat raisins for seasick
to guard against risk
unknown fever, inexplicable vanishings & you were right
I am overtaken. Not with the damp
eighty-degree nights, or this bare living
over blue water, dragging my nets
through Milton's seas, regions of Chaos & Anarchy,
supping on gulls' eggs, skulls of gulls
tapped open with geologic hammer; not
the dead Indians or the murdering, daggering, gun-toting
    Gauchos, or even
the death splash on one's friends, the shipwrecked men; not
a black squall so terrible the fright leaks into your boots
as the shaking ship pitches over
in the dark & all you know quickly fills with water—no—
I prayed then, Father, I must admit, to be saved
but not from these things.

Father, the one who constantly leaves, who risks all
possible constancy
known love, intimate human company
cast adrift on the planet, perhaps never to return again;
the one who will barter these things
for reckless, immeasurable, uncertain outcomes,
is he selfish or brave?

You will be happy to hear
Humboldt's jungles have proved bigger than fear
& as unfathomable as the sharp, elongated groves
of waxen, cupping, almost ridiculous flowers
or the wakeful birds in the wood, chorusing words you've
        never heard
the burr & chirrup all around. You want to chirrup too
to screech this language you don't yet speak
to give it tongue but the vanishing
vanishes then, or you do, swallowed if not whole
than wholly. Whatever use for the forms of these flowers
I have not yet found, but in myself
a new use, a freedom of form, I am
somehow newborn, or will keep on chiselling
my poor notations for astonishment.

No nebulous nothing this might be
no prosaic imaginary, just the raw, incarnate
stuff of the world. What is
Absolute is the way I stand here undone

an Englishman among insect-angels in the rain
all ploy now paid, rain
pouring down my trunk & the tree I shelter beneath,
the entwining that engulfs like sleep;
inside some great aching silence, yes,
this man is vanishing.

I have watched the Godful men unload
their crates of porcelain, wine-glasses, fine linen
& their savages, Christian-converted
onto the naked beach, each one carrying
an end of the new mahogany table
over the waves to the place where, in winter, they believe
the men sometimes eat their women.
I see home is blind
bears blind poets whose dreams of paradise, however much
        I love them,
come from losing it.

Yet I have traded home, safety, my old ways for the way
the light falls over blue Acacia trees, for the smell
of Passiflora on warm wind, & the oranges
Father, are orange, not green.
I have traded these things as you might a coin for a cocoa nut
which once you've broken open, drunk its white
milk, chewed its soft fruit, you know you can never go back
to apples.

The Diodem, the inflatable, ever-inverted fish I caught
near the shore here, stains carmine any man who touches it.
You see, I have dipped
this parchment to give you my new tint. Father,
I might weep.

But truth is, if I were Milton, I'd spend the last of my light here.
I'd withstand the inevitable lunacy of the chase,
the chance of vanishing at the hands
of the bandit, the Gaucho, hands soaked in blood;
for exile, though impermanent in time
is rarely impermanent within.

I'd forsake everything
even you
for one glimpse again of that forest
stewing in the rain.

Blue Vapour

He took from Wordsworth
the thought
that what was remote
unreachable in science
were 'proper objects
of the poet's art'
& Charles believed this
keen in heart: that
science (by that meant
the mysteries of knowing)
might become, not rote,
but *'sufficiently habitual*
to become poetical.'

At times, he imagined William
beside him
rootless and roving
shoes creaking through the low brush,
a kindred spirit in wisdom won
through words alone.

He stopped by a copper creek
to write:
'I, a geologist,
have ill-defined
notion of land covered with ocean,
former animals, slow
force cracking surface &c—
truly poetical.'

William ambled
but stayed ahead
while Charles
red-hot with spiders
in a fidget
of linen & delight
& writing notes faster
than he could write, was glad
to be alone with views.

Poetry was a song
but science an immense solitude.

And yet, Poetry comes quickly
he knew
to the soul of all
who site it. Charles did.
The slam of blue
when the deep unbelievable valley
finally hits you
the cliff edge just the beginning
of light.

William dove off the mountain
cascading into blue vapour
while the tangle
of Charles's darkest and widest problem

his burgeoning secret
was wild & snagging
& as slow to free
as his thighs from
the high bramble of fern.

When he turned around
it and he
murky as the distracted air
seemed abruptly erased
no longer there.

How to Geologise Abroad

He chipped
at hillocks.

Hammer-tapped
slaty sandstone
scales of mica
granite, veins
of feldspar & quartz.

Humboldt (of course)
had been here before

but Charles would leave
his own score

the beat of a mallet
defeating the cleavage of eons

ferruginous stone
abounding with fossils.

All around him
slow toil: Snow
Volcano, Earthquake
Thunder Storms.

He could hear the *plinging*
of little molten tears
the red lapilli lava had left
falling through the air

welding the animals in.

Rio, June, 1832

The minuscule spider he met
near Botafogo Bay
was a cataleptic stowaway on the silk
thread of another
scavenging the sticky haul.
Like a child caught
with its hand in the sweet jar
as soon as Charles's eyes clamped
onto its ruse
it froze, feigned fast death
& fell off. What hard work
he thought, dragging his net, this life
of homelessness, pretence & pinch
to be the thief who leaps
from the building
to save on a bit of web-spinning.

Jungle

started about ½ after six.
& passed over scorching plains
therm: in pocket 96°.—
lost our way
             – C.D., Field Notebook

Too much tea by dawn
the sugar slapped him to sluggish shock
his pulse was both too slow & too quick
sunlight on the white sand too thickly laid
& the stunted trees offered no shade.

He trailed a brackish trickle of water
into the forest, but he couldn't see
from the glare or from
the tangled lairs of snaking
reaching carnivorous green. The creek
out of the corner of his eye
was a slithering silver strap
too sharp to look at directly.
Only in the shadows where the light
fogged the water in opal patches
pressed with tree-ferns
fronds pooling
at the bottom, could he discern
the rippling of morning.

The darkest parts of the jungle then
matched his mind; curved ferns bending
over an ancient water course,
Lepidoptera of thoughts hovering
at the edges of consciousness.
But he couldn't hold onto them
couldn't hold his pencil, couldn't see straight.
He tripped over rotten logs, thrashed at parasitical plants
the low, spiky native leaves through his sleeve
as though he were being leached with pins.
The air nickered with crickets, giant insects.
He blazed under rolled-up trousers, cotton shirt.
How could anything think in a country this hot?

The Brazilians, dexterous with blades
soon took their swords to the creepers
hacked back vines & trunks
& bearded monkeys
still clinging to trees
fell

Forms for Rapture

In the ringing forests of Brazil
even the frogs came out for evening song,
matched the crickets in chant
& lit by the flashing green matter
of fireflies, recalled to him the bright
heartbreak of Malibran.

Stunned still until he catches
one winged, nocturnal beetle
a pulsing emerald in cupped palms.
He watches the light within. Inner
radiance is impossible
to conceal. Beryl & chromium
chemical organs, forms
for rapture.

Charles studies firefly courtship
the intermittent patterned flares that call out
through the night; he marvels at how simple
it could be, not hats & dance cards
just the incandescent flaunting song from afar—
come find me.

He suspects that passion too
gives man new
faculties akin
to the suckered feet
of the singing jungle frog

as it crawls perfectly vertically
up a pane of glass when captured;
or to the larvae of a *Lampyris:*
luminiferous organs
of attachment.

Even when the firefly
is decapitated it retains
its brightness, its shining
sticky fluid & every slight touch
prior to death only amplifies
the intensity of its light.

Darwin's Noah

The dead animals were swinging
in his cabin; staring, stinking
sloshing jars, hanging by rafter
coming after him, awaiting
their final honours
eyes wide and blank with last moments.

Too seasick to dissect, he pictured Noah
not as Biblical hero
but as a man with a job to do;
his brain full of Chronometrical Measurements
navigational notations
trying to catch a snatch of sleep
while the ark hurled and tossed in the torrents
and the sun above turned black.

He saw Noah and his family
cramped and bickering in their tiny
gopherwood compartment
while the animals stamped
and cried nearby
terrified;
while the seeping scent of half-digested
animal suppers, stomach acid and shit
flowed freely beneath his door,
a river of sick.

A rogue bolt of lightning
split the waters and his wife's hair lit green.

His sons and their wives were screaming
their lips stretched wide round the fright
though silent under the deafening
(for he would never hear God's words as well again)
as they plunged into the open mouths
of flood-bearing, record-breaking waves.

His hurriedly cobbled boat
threatened to smash open
for he'd been too busy
walking with God
to pay much attention to carpentry.

On the second and third decks
the animals had begun
to eat each other.

He could hear the shrieks, the screech
the smash of fox beneath the panicked
rhino's foot, the tiger tearing red flesh
off the deer that pressed into the corner
where a snake slowly wrapped
its black weight around a mouse
whose twitching, pink nose reddened
with sudden blood.

Noah, being Noah, would have prayed.
But only for so long.

He was a man with a hefty job to do:
keep order where there was none
save some creeping pairs for posterity and deliver
his children alive, for already
the bears were beginning to claw
at the cabin door.

He vowed that if he lived to see new land
and his wife and his sons lived
and the wives of his sons lived
he would willingly build an altar
on which he would slaughter
every bird, every animal and every creeping thing
as offerings

and over time
eat the rest.

On the Subject of Untimely Extinction

Though *Elephas maximus* had survived, old shaggy Mastodon
suffered a fateful extinguishment, Captain Fitzroy enlightened,
due to the door of the ark being cut much
too small for its four sworded tusks.
Darwin could just see it
like a massive, ancient Highland cow
one brown eye peering through the slit in its knotted fringe;
he could hear its bellowing deep *mawww*
as it watched from shore the flood waters rush in,
the boat float off without him.

El Naturalista

He placed one Promethean
between his lips, struck quick the wooden stick to spark
against his teeth & watched
the brown eyes widen
voices rapturise to see
a man make flame burst
from his jaws. He couldn't speak
spur & dagger-tongues, but kept
stores of such match gadgetry
in his vest pocket to pass
safely across the pampas & cactus lands
like a pale, clothed, combustible Titan
some kind of human cannon
while the broad-hatted men turned him round
in wonder, searching
for his wick.

Down the Backbone

1.

Captain Cook said the closest thing he could compare
their language to was a man clearing his throat.

To be sure, these sounds are more croaky than a cough
but nothing much to listen to, a kind of whirrup
and gutting mew, a husky gruff
of the tongue over the soft palate.
These Fuegians pull faces, pull our beards
try to be taller than us
and do not understand what we can have possibly done
with our women.

They are happy to dance anyway.
On the beach, we tip hats
and together—copper skins and Englishmen—
the *Beagle's* boldest sailors waltz
waltz away the morning.

2.

Here, down the knobbly backbone of South America
we trade our crimson cloth
for fish, a long nail for fish;
we try to trade everything
for fish or crabs

and what we do not trade they grab
thinking the white man foolish
for giving away such fine treasure
for a simple supper.

They rip the crimson cotton
and share it around
knot it into hair.

Silly savages don't understand
that they'll only get ahead
in this world
by hoarding.

3.

The once-enscuffled, once-captured, newly-Anglicised trio:
York Minister, Fuegia Basket, Jemmy Button
have returned
in hat and gloves, carrying their Bibles and china
to the raw
unseamed edge of the world.

Their barbarian kin
a dozen rabid savage men
black-faced, white-banded, animal-skinned
laugh their heads off.

Though I'm beginning to believe that both
the highest and lowest
forms of man, evidenced here, are of one
tree, one great stem
of humanity, it is not yet clear to me
how a Fuegian becomes a Newton.

The efforts to teach them
to talk and pray, to button a waistcoat, to eat
with knife and fork from blue china plates
have proved the true improvability of man,
his ultimate plasticity, a sort of
self-transmutation.

Yet why is it I
in my beard and worn breeches, that seems to be
the alien species?

4.

Our boat met hers by the shore.

I'd never seen a woman
entirely unclothed before
and found it deplorable
though strangely thrilling
how she let the sleet and rain fall
onto her body, silvering her red skin

her notched spine, the black
shag of hair over her eyes.
Her curious dark eyes did not flinch.

Unruffled by cold she trawled
twitching the line
into the canoe, her breasts flapping,
then tore out the abdomens
of tiny fish with her teeth
to clean them.

Never before
a woman so naked.
Never before an animal
so female.

What was the protocol
in the midst of such nakedness
in bobbing boats side by side
while men exchange mimicries like chatter.
To look? To not look?
To look through entirely
as though entirely absent?
That's what the others did.

My hand could trail the water.
Could reach over, grasp the rough edge
of her bark canoe, could touch.

I did not want the sailors
to see me blush.

Paddling off, I could not help
but turn, compelled
by her flesh, so mortal,
so visibly fragile.
Though no mirror reflected me—
she looked back.

5.

In a year we find Jemmy Button
has returned to his old ways.
He's shed his clothes for his bare
base soul, claiming old happiness
in fruits and fish.

We redress him and feed him one last time
sit him down for a good chat
while his new little wife cries.

Doesn't he want to go back to England?

Well no.

He's made arrowheads
out of bone. His gift back.

When the boat floats out of sight
his head bends to soft silence
the sadness of his wife.

Jemmy builds a fire on the sand.
The smoke curls, waves goodbye.

The Tortoise

Darwin rides the back of the giant
Galapagos tortoise, *Testudo Indicus*
so slowly across the hot sand
he can nearly count the grains he passes.

Its claws dent the beach
unflinching at lava rocks' scorching heat;
one after the other

up the well-trod path
to the waterhole

resolute, unwavering purpose.

The curved bulk
of its body

wipes clean
any prints.

When he first perched astride the shelled reptile
he rapped its chequered back
hello? Heard the dull, polished echo
within

as it then stood & began
its slow climb
snacking on cactus
& lichen

passing *salinas*
in sandstone craters
where the skull
of one sealing captain once fell.

It does not seem to mind
its passenger.

The black volcanic sand
the distant mud
the smell of the sea
leap over them.

Rope

Sometimes the tip of a long rope pierced his shirt
through to his heart and knotted there.
A tangled mess of strands pulled tight
while the other end uncoiled down to his boots
slithered across the deck, slung the rail of the brig
and bobbed and sunk, wet and loose, wave over wave
across the sea like some determined snake,
a hawser back to his lost house in England. Sometimes,
he would wake in his hammock with it tugging, not always gently
and feel the broad hands of his father, the six
ivory hands of his sisters, one over the other,
towing him up onto the deck across the swabbed midnight floors
    on his back
slowly, certainly, hauling him backwards
to the squeak, stretch and fray
of the cord's plaited lace, the tough weave that wrenched him
towards the water. He'd have to yank back hard
feet bracing against the rails, shred the hot
skin from his palms
as he tried to tie himself to the chock, resisting
the force that would tear his breast in two
and carry him home.

The sound this colossal tussle made was the sound
of an old ship six weeks crossing the South Pacific, wood shrinking
and swelling in elemental stare. As he attuned
his cold terror to the infinite
curve of the Earth, his hull was hardening
against the henpeck of family.

One night he took his blade and severed the towrope
close to the chest, watched as the ragged end slunk
one last time across the polished ship
and slipped over the edge. He had to listen hard to hear the splash.
The sawn knot he cauterised with a match
until its filaments melted and fused, making
a warm, raised, pocket-shaped wound.

Falls at Weatherboard, Australia, January 17th, 1836

Darwin stood on the brink
of the bay, mid-day
under forty-three degree sun
stunned by the unexpected
drop, from such a thin
rill of water—what
a thrill! to find it this high
above the sea, such deep shores
laid dry & sown across
the bottom with seams of trees.

On wind-worked rock
he sat & wrote & waited
as if he were on the worn stone benches
of an Athenian amphitheatre
for a chorus of Clouds & Birds
& saw bays forming before him by songs of water
not seas; a lyric of rain in slow eons
that fell note by note
& noting the time it took
to walk the creek back & how far
yet to travel before dark, he took
leave of this play, of the blue haze
& all those loud white *Coccatoos*.

But if he'd stayed
& stood on that spot until dawn
he would have seen
how the blue floats down

how the fog rises up to bring back
the secret sea (the open palm
of a conductor's hand lifting
to lure the music) as that masked choir
of white and black feathered players
scream back to their leaves
& in their place, a host
of diamonds takes the stage
to call
the moon out—
an *exodos* of light
whose solitude was his own
whose grace is silence.

Handel, January 17th, 1836

In the shadow of an ancient cave
under the curved, ferned roof of rock
after a snack of salted beef
Darwin dozed
though only briefly
in a heavy jacket of heat

while Handel's *Messiah* rose
like a bubble from the deep
& soared cliff-high behind his eyes
an ascending thought
he could not capture.

He had the truest sense
that there was so much more
to man than breath.

He dreamed his inner body
stretched to accommodate the vast
reaches of mind, stretched
across the empty, remembered wastes
of Patagonia & its stark opposite:
the hungry hands of the dark
Tierra del Fuegians
their yammerschoonering after the brass buttons
on his coat;
& how his own hand reached hungrily
after the teeming, secret life
of this country

for he too wanted so much more
than he could speak.

His throat was parched with sleep.
A trickle of sweat creeked
down his brow
& cheek & he could transfer it
to his tongue
like a lizard
with one quick flickering Hallelujah reach.

Moments of adaptation were just breaths
in the history of the world
in the body of the world.

Charles woke, stood, stretched
& broke wind. He glimpsed
between hanging leaves
how each step he took
through his mind's thousand voices
marked a moment when the liquid note
of thought might hatch like an aria
into something altogether new.

While he'd watched the waterfall slide down the rocks
in random, but seemingly determined configurations,
he pictured his branching diagram
of life, still misty as a dream
which he had only just begun

to sketch in his mind;
it matched the first catch of bramble
in the hand as he ambled along this creek
or a map of enemy movements
(the bird stalking the slick, mocha lizard over the stone)
or indeed, the long, river-twisted
gullet of man

& the possibility struck him
'we may all be netted together'.
The chorus rose in him, too
like one of Handel's harmonies & he sang
back its unadmitted prayer
May we all be netted together
for it was suddenly inconceivable to him
that the universe could be
just a state of accumulating chances.

Survival was an act of consciousness
& yet you could only do
so much
about it.

How much happier
one was in the sunlight
in the glare of this afternoon light
just to let life
strike you open
to let it go, to flow

creek-like
in the company of a thousand, competing creature voices
towards the exhilarating
the inevitable
falling.

Return to Weatherboard,
January 24–25th, 1836

There was smoke
fire was everywhere.
In the burning woodlands
the *'never failing eucalyptus'*
were failing
to sustain the flames.
Darwin rode the solitary road
cut into the sandstone plain
back from Bathurst, the lost
cockatoos of the world
screaming.

By night, the dark blue clouds
had gathered over the amphitheatre
of stone that the sky threatened again to fill.
The white bones of the trees
shone through thin mist
the air was cold & comfortless & still.

All the next day he lay unwell
in a prison of drizzle
at the Weatherboard Inn.

How much worse than flame
were the reflective, skulking fingers of fog
the silent ghosts of the trees
the dripping eaves.

Even the birds today
didn't once call.

The Sailor

Though the crew called him Philosopher,
his pleasure was to secretly think
of himself as sailor. Hadn't he
learnt to eat canister meat & lemon juice;
to sleep in a hammock slung over a table
in a cabin eleven feet by ten
with a fourteen year old midshipman & maps
in pitches & gales; to toss
out his net in the dark & cart
the sea trove back luminous with dust;
to sit on deck or boom on warm nights
acquainting himself with sailors' doubts
about Moses. They knew a boat
was mere wood in the face of true flood
& they'd all more likely end up on the seabed
than safe on dry land, for they had seen
the endlessness of water.

He was sailor as he worked at Astronomy
or at the proud, white slap of sail
one line in hand, one locked in teeth
as they tacked into port past flying fish
& porpoises; but truth was
his shirts were marked: DARWIN.
He shared cabin meals with the Captain
& never could cure his seasickness
or that salty thirst from swallowing sea
that made him dream he drank his samples clean
while the creatures rasped dry between two sheets of paper,

until by the end of that sorrowful, long fraction of his life
he hated every wave of the everlasting ocean.

Out of sync with time itself, by nature
he did not live well in the present
but loved to spend the still hours
conceiving castles of the past
or drunk on dream's anticipations
& he was a dockside vulture with letters.

While he believed when he would at last land
on English sand, he'd want to stuff a pipe
with pound notes & smoke his joy—
there was only mud & rain
& disenchantment's shame
to greet him. The perpetual seesawing
the desert of water
he was only too happy to be rid of
but of that feverish land
he'd never walk through again
which his sisters called 'odious South America',
he had just hot pictures in his heart.
Words, watercolours would not fix them
in his mind forever.

From the man he'd been
to the man he had become—
ship & sea—that five-year orbit of globe
was the most magnificent present

tense, a perpetual birthday bridge
between two people called Charles.

But he quickly gleaned that no one wanted
too much of his Southern happinesses.
He learned not to talk of the secret passion
for pineapples his tongue
would long for, or how once
he had shat, what appeared upon close look
to be a new kind of beetle, but was simply
the passing of his very first passionfruit seed.

And he'd never mention
how that large, extinct, fossilised skull,
a *Megatherium* he'd unearthed from Punta Alta & carted home—
now plopped awkwardly beside him in the parlour,
silent, sullen, brazen bone
as his sisters passed teacups & judgement
on vexing persons turned into nice little wives—
was himself.

On those nights wrapped in white sheets
as starchly rippled as jibs
he'd remember dining on ostriches
& dozing Gaucho-fashion
in the open camp with a concert of cicadas
& sand that chirped when you walked across it
so hot you could feel its colour
with closed eyes.

The good sisterhood at home
thought they'd got their Charley back
but nightly, as the ten-gun brig loomed large
he felt the Mount's rooms pitch and tip.

Though he did what he must
in terms of life and wife
his brain was never again the same.
His dreams now came to him
in waves of intense scarlet.

– III –

"Odious dirty smokey town."

– C.D., 1837

London (I)

1.

The soot & fog of dawn streets
the dark filth of snowy streets, the long
quiet white lengths of them
lined with little squares of yellow;
the glitter of streets at first light
when the snow's just fallen.

It's possible to feel new, now, here.
Possible for something previously unseen to sneak
past the gates of yourself, just a glimpse
of something, you won't put your finger on it,
not quite; a forest of pines you finally find
an entrance to, a dark place between two trees
where you might slip through
into a moss-strewn place. There's no need to hurry
in your well-pressed suit, your shined boots
nodding your head to the men you pass
lifting your hat to the ladies, bowing at the waist;
no need to mind the minutes
winding your watch to the boot step
for *is this not a second?*
Is that, not the time?

2.

The march of men
& the shouts of men
in the ante meridian
the working men, the gentlemen
these clean free souls
with cogs to attend
& wives to bend
the precision of their buttoned shoes
in twos and fours, before
the clatter of flies & coaches.

The parasols opening
with a rush and snap
the silk stretching over
the creak-back frames
fluttering skyward, bat-like,
fifth-limbed & lame, satin
slippers gliding over the lisp
of trampled streets.

3.

The postman with his small squares of loss & solace,
the flower peddler with her painted lips, already old for her age,
the lawyer with neat moustache, will slit his throat this evening,
the gin-swilling, skirt-chasing varmint
dragging a shadow of debt, selling his love poems,
the butler who passes houses as if about to answer their doors,
the second sons & every single eligible daughter
hoping to be given a second look,
the *poco curante*, dreamy eyes, just walked through horse shit,
the woman with book in hand, never sits still for portraits,
the town crier with his black whip to better chastise the ladies
        of pleasure,
the fop with a pocket of withered nosegay & one last witty
        thing to say,
the aristocrat with his family purse & a vicarage to choose,
the Naturalist with his net, tone-deaf, carting specimens,
        singing for beetles,
the Politician & the Reverend trying to staunch insurrection
like blood from sudden wounds,
the heretic looking for happiness in this world, not the next,
The Times with their CAPITAL PUNISHMENTS,
the chemist with his tests and crucibles
his instructions: the soul
of each man & woman should be
pushed back inside the tiny tube, back down.

4.

If you go out at dawn
mind the minutes
before the slush breaks
the hush, the rupture of carts
carrying bodies to hospital
& bodies to the medical school
to be strapped & hacked & sliced & sawed & emptied
blood flowing down
into the bucket of sawdust on the floor.

John Gould, Superintendent of Stuffed Birds

The gardener's son at Windsor Castle
as a child collected
the soft meadow froth of dandelions
for Queen Caroline's tea.

He married his way out of poverty
by bedding a painter
& painted his way out of poverty
by selling his portraits of birds
his wife had hand-tinted.

He laid the world
& its birds
out
on the table in imperial
folio-sized plates.

He, who had loved
but had never seen
a live hummingbird

still hummed as he worked.
He untangled beak from beak—
Cactus-finch from Woodpecker finch
Darwin's Galapagos 'wrens' & 'blackbirds'
that were all really forms of finches—
in the basement rooms of the Zoological Society
where sometimes he swore he heard
bird song in the water-pipes.

Darwin was late the first time they met.
Some of the feathers on his specimens
were bent back from bad packing
more than several had no labels.
He'd paid more mind to the rocks
than to the birds, though he chattered
rather like one.

Later, Gould took
his dark, banded eyes
his beaked nose to America to finally see
the ruby-throated hummingbird:

a splash of iridescent red paint beneath the beak,
the bright green back, the black-bladed wings
gifted with acrobatic dances.

He'd dashed out hundreds of sketches
of the bird from his mind

but nothing had prepared him
for the wound-up bird-toy before him
this tiny, hovering winged thing
a plush, beating palmful that even
his most childlike self
could not have invented

nor its tree-nests of bud scales
roofed in lichen & tied
with spider's silk;
nests lined with the down
of dandelions.

He was a child again with them
ruby-throated remembering
the sticky silk purse
of metamorphosed flowers that mere breath
could disperse

the clinging white seeds in his hair
the Queen's stare from the window.

And like a child, he tried
to hustle two birds home
in coat pockets to comfort him.

They died.

Metaphysical Thoughts, Con't

He thought he could believe
ever clearly
in the free will of an oyster
& how it could produce
beneficial changes to the oyster body,
oyster organisation over time—

if mammals have free will
as they no doubt do
it is obvious to see
then an oyster too...

But what would be
the free will of an oyster?
he wondered
staring out at the last
of the day's light.

Darwin was no ostreaphile
but had dined often with his brother on some
washed down with champagne
& with his sisters at Bournemouth
as a child once, & had felt directly
he should take a dissecting knife
to the hinged fawn moons of flesh
& harvest complete some primordial story.
But many times after, beached off the *Beagle*,
he'd had late-baked feasts of cracking shells
on warm sand & had almost learned the knack

for the circular slide of the knife in his hand
& the slick listless gift of the sea
that slipped down his throat
its aftertaste of fish & algae
& something else…
what, he did not know.

Rather like swallowing
one's own tongue, in fact.

Captain Fitzroy, too, had been most partial
to oysters at the table, but when asked
by Darwin about the free will of the shells
spewed forth by the Earth
into the highest inland elevations

or the oyster bed
he'd discovered in Chiloé
that grew a giant forest
350 feet above sea

Fitzroy spoke not of geology
but instead said
he'd make a Few Remarks
Concerning God's Great Deluge.

Yes, Darwin explained impatiently.
The deluge of seawater
after *earthquake or volcanic activity.*

But Fitzroy by this time
had long gone to bed
dousing ship lights promptly
each night at 8:30 p.m.

Charles looked over his notes.
The free will (if so called) in oyster...
he continued, but then, loss of heart
wasn't so sure of the sense.

Surely if the oyster had free will
it would will itself
never to be eaten again
& definitely not by
tongues of such oyster blasphemy
as God-fearing Fitzroy's?

Might be some mistake of logic.
Would be grateful if somebody
would advise.

London (II)

He curls on his air cushions
on the floor of his brother's house

wintery drizzle reason enough
to stay another day in bed with his book.

The gloom drifts up from the street
it's always there, sweet sometimes

like flowers dying
or old socks writhing

sour on the floor.
He throws his pair across the room

& sinks down, hoarding
the brief hours of light

when there's so much left to read
feet tucked, hot-gutted with tea

& something he might call longing.
Elusive, mid-day melancholy.

The low abdominal ache, the salty sweat scent
of his own skin unnerves him

as he turns pages, secretly
wanting to embrace, to enfold her, somehow

unable to stop: *"And thus died*
MISS CLARISSA HARLOWE
in the blossom of her youth
and beauty: and who,
her tender years considered,
has not left behind her her superior
in extensive knowledge
and watchful prudence;
nor hardly her equal
for unblemished virtue
exemplary piety
sweetness of manners
discreet generosity
and true Christian charity:
and these all set off by the most
graceful modesty
and humility;
yet on all proper occasions
manifesting a noble presence
of mind and true magnanimity:
so that she
may be said to have been
not only an ornament to her sex,
but to human nature."

The bones in his long legs, now flung
over the edge of the bed, stretch & sigh with that

light.
All that is woman.

Soon, when the smoky hints of sun & young women appear
opening doors & stepping

out under their parasols
like wet flowers

he'll tear himself from his book
of delicious misery, sit

in the window
& watch them sway past

trying to glimpse faces
under the bells of black silk

wondering which one
he might catch

as she plummets from the sky
like a shot bird.

36 Great Marlborough St.

There was, however, the unfinished
business of his list. Each night, when
the new gas lamps were lit, he returned to it
taking, after beef steak & tea, a clean sheet
of paper to his desk on which to more clearly
formulate the question.

Though he suspected in many
of life's matters only
the most fit subsisted, was one
such as he, in fact, fit
for this? The lamps flickered
through smoky, yellow air
their assent or dispute, he could not tell.
His riddle hovered there like a halo
& the image of his aloneness, a kind of eternal
aloneness he was only beginning to fully grasp,
produced a sensation of fear in him
akin to heart failure.

In a column under *For*, he wrote:
I suspect there exists
a degree of warmth greater
than I have previously known, pleasure
beyond exercise & birds singing.
I suspect there is a pleasure
that in its perfect form
combines somehow all three things—

Hot-cheeked he crushed
& tossed his paper.
Dipped his pen. Began again.

Against—
'I shall never go up in a balloon.'

His days now in his scribbler's den
just a daze of volumes, sheets, sentences,
no company, no society, no sun
& certainly no balloons
were glimpsed in that sooty sky
as he crawled his thoughts along the strata
ignoring the radiant matter he suspected
beneath his Earth's crust.

Oh the trampling of paper
though extravagant, gave distinct pleasure too.

Again, he dipped.
For—
but stopped short.

The fire popped. His servant
Syms moved through the next room.

For wasn't Charles, truthfully, no more than a working bee,
a neuter bee, some kind of half-man

creeping like a caterpillar on his many little legs
on his short, spotted, spindly legs
along the crowded black streets, glimpsing
the white lace of white petticoats
fluttering above him, leaving him
breathless with their proximity
in the most unphilosophical
uncaterpillar-like manner?

And a caterpillar, it must be said
couldn't catch, much less feed
a butterfly.

Charles would pace all night til he got it.
He was free, he was free
to work, mutter, drink brandy in wild, solitary surmise,
ride, philosophise, talk aloud & toss paper—
Wasn't he?

In the morning, a bewildered Syms
would find him crumpled & curled
on the sofa in foetal sleep, twenty
scrawled & balled pages like snowballs on the floor.
He would stoop & lift them all
carefully uncreasing them
over the edge of the windowsill to reuse
himself later. The last sheet
lay on the desk, clean, unfinished,

as if its three choked words
had prematurely exhausted their author:

"Marry—Marry—Marry."

Is This Not Our House?

I found its empty rooms
not quite empty—
the loose ends of other lives,
the odd yellow curtains, the odd
blue walls, the dead dog in the garden
which I removed, but not without first
trying to ascertain
what had killed it.

The drawing room
where we'll draw
out the happy geese
of mutual speech, the circling
of my feet there on rainy days.
There's more light
at the back, more quiet
in this part of town
& I shall hear you better
than I can from here.

The black sparrows I watch in the garden,
the melting snow,
the mahogany piano,
the clanging pots & pans,
the drawers of shells I carefully carry
in by hand, the new white curtains,
the whistle of Euston Station,
the cook caught for 14 pounds
& 14 shillings with tea & sugar,

the ever-black soot in the sky,
our neighbour, the Shakespearean clown, two doors down,
the rooms red & green as if painted by parrots,
& my specimen museum
in the front attic, creature-beasts
like private gargoyles crouching
above our church, the mews at the back
where coachmen sing.

Sometimes we'll eat walnut pickle & stewed pear
& sometimes muffin pudding.

Is this not our house
where you & I lie in our still
mysteriously perfect bodies
where you play your long fingers
over the chords of my skin.
Is this not the house
you will humanise me in?
Outside, the December wind
howls as if to knock us down.
Inside, we will huddle
the fire near, nights like this,
all the nights of our green green life.

Your buttered eggs on toast,
your broth, hot and brown, brought
to me on the sofa when I am sick,
your footsteps on the stairs,

a long chestnut strand of your hair
on my pillow, the drip
of your pen across
rough paper, your kiss,
your voice in the kitchen with the cook
you will sack, 'too cute', the way you look
as you scold me, while laughing.

And when on our first night we drew
the awful curtains in the windows
of our terraced house closed
I could only hear
your breath
shallow as I stepped closer, I couldn't
get close enough
quick enough.

I don't care
if the floors are hardened mud
or the windows without glass
or if our chairs are carved from the roughest wood
& the bed sags in the middle
as long as you are there with me my Em,
as long as you are there.

In the Pantry

3 jars Raspberry jam
12 bottles Ginger beer
1 pigeon pie
6 pots of lemon pickle
8 pots of walnut pickle
1 head of pickling pig
4 jars cranberry sauce
3 small muffin puddings
5 mammalia in spirits of wine
3 jars orange jelly
4 jars apple jelly
5 jars marmalade
1 burrowing mole
2 pots cold cream with hint of rose water
7 bottles of gooseberries
10 preserved eggs
1 bat
1 box of snap gingerbread buttons
1 barking bird with larvae of beetles in stomach
1 mince pie
1 mouse
1 head of mouse
& 12 shells
sold in the market
at Buenos Aires
for spoons

December 27th, 1839

The red notebook:

Lat: 51° 28′ 38″N
230 Fathoms deep

Caught by a hook
my first specimen
of genus squalus.

Body: *Blueish White to Skimmed Milk White*
Its eyes the most beautiful things I ever knew.

Pupils: *Scotch Blue, like throat of blue titmouse*
but with the lustre of a jewel appearing like a sapphire.
Though now it sleeps.

Touching
foot with sheet of paper
suddenly
produced jerk, curl of toes.
Squalled without tears.

Good spec. for testing
the limits of inheritance—
& emotion in man.

I could not exactly see the heart
but felt mine skip.

Squalus Darwinii !!!
I cried
but my wife insists:

William Erasmus.

– IV –

"I long for to-morrow.
I feel sure I shall become deeply attached to Down."

– C.D., 1842

Coralline

1.

Charles would never forget the limb of vital life
Professor Sedgwick
first planted in his mind;
a spring of water that flowed
from a chalk hill
and left an elegant tracery of lime
in brushwork lines on twigs.
This bubbling cave of transmutation
Stendhal then turned to a staff of salt jewels
before his eyes
into which longing itself had crystallised.

Darwin, The Eager, had searched the source
and not satisfied with mere twig
had uprooted and flung an entire bush into the brook
hoping to come back
as love-caked as that
branching bone
he pulled from the water's spell.

2.

When love finally came
it accreted slowly,
gathering particle by particle

yet within a week it seemed
like the sheltered cave
of a shallow atoll
glittering with sand and sun
enclosing him
and he called her, his one,
coralline.

3.

They built their home
on the chalk downs
a silt bed of shell and bone
calcium carbonate
and filled the powdery rooms with stone
marble, wood, velvet, silk, calico.
They filled the pillows with down
feathers and papered the walls
with delicate mosaics
of petal and leaf, violet and rose.

Still the house soon grew
coralline too
spawning new babies and bodies
crystallising into a solid shape
regular, geometric as a frozen snowflake
a grain of salt
this colourless, time-telling, gem-encrusted form that love filled.

4.

A father and his four children, coral-handed, bandits all, take
     turns
strapping the magnifying glass across their eyes,
shuffling along the dining room wall
in search of Earth's most infinitesimal meanings
and the flicker of minutes
caught within the paper
enlarging to 300 times the power of the eye
the pale petrified postures
and skeletons of tiny sea creatures
fossilised beneath the flowers,
preserved in chalk.

The children will ever afterwards
believe their house to be a giant barnacle
clinging to a buoy that sinks and rises again
with the weight of accretion,
some kind of sea-seeking
crystal palace. They lick
the north window panes on windy days
for the taste of salt.

Indeed, on winter nights the house windows glow
like Thompson's phosphorescence,
imperfectly known luminous points
on a raft of black sky;

yet when he sees them from the outside
the yellow lamps in his wife Emma's,
in his children's bedroom windows
he thinks
yes,
there is light
of the softest and most destructible tenderness.

5.

Love, love, our architectonic
is neither plant nor mineral
but both
neither animal nor island
but both
neither male nor female
but both
neither hard nor soft
but both
neither solitary nor colony
but both
neither fragile nor robust
but both
neither this nor that
and so both. And so all.
Microscopic, telescopic, generative,
we are home, architect and inhabitant;

love how we propagate
brain and branching
how we grow
from broken stems.

6.

And though she secretly hopes
you two will be for each other forever
you know
love will last as long as you last;
that you will return
to fossil, to salt, to chalk-
bones, your new home geology's strata
and your veins, your life force
will turn to quartz
your fingers to fossils, your brain
will become rock.
Soon, we too will be
wallpaper, my coralline.

The Names for Things

We are drifters three, through Down Woods
in spacious lengths unmeasured
by foot or time
temporarily misplaced
in dim shadow, caves
of hazel, clay stuck to boots
in great running clumps.
Beyond the yelling distance.

There are names for things here.
We do not know them all.

Later, unbooting
on the back stairs, sucking whole oranges
beside the parlour's marble fire
sweet conflations of orange
juice & licking flame.

When bees halo the lime trees
Papa is on his back
under his Panama hat
on the brown grass
telling long stories

about the names for things.
We remember everything.

Behind heavy curtains we heft the books,
open them over the red-flowered floor.

We line up word against word against word:
editions, dictionaries, directories, maps,
trying to identify, to recognise,
classifying affinities
with him.

The clack of billiard balls
in the billiard room next door
sounds like heads to us,
round rolling skulls
sinking into the green felt pockets
where secret things are kept.

We huddle in the closet under the stairs
with the coats & mallets
take turns reciting the names for things.
They will not remember us back.

After the last
ice puddles of the year are cracked
he will come & collect us
specimens in his cupped palm,
peer down ever gently & carry us
deep into the names for things.

He will find
the open purple faces
the insect eyes of wild orchids among the junipers,
teach us the true meaning of holy.

The Sparrow

broke its neck
against the parlour window,
soaring too fast round the corner
of the house. He'd seen it
strike the glass;
gone before it hit the ground.
It only took a second.

How dangerous & haphazard
the world was.
He was frequently amazed
that a person was not made obsolete before supper
much less had lived thirty-seven years—
thirteen thousand, five-hundred & fourteen days
in a row without pause.

Was it luck that got one through life?
Narrow escape? Was it wit or strength,
was survival just a *jolly-good* slap
on the back & likewise
did those that die lack
inherent determination, a *laissez-faire*
approach to daily existence?

When Emma played Bach's
The Sheep May Graze Safely
he could not feel joy at her
light-hearted plucking at the notes

nor feel her relief that God was near;
he could only hear the wolf
in the field, silently stalking.

Sometimes, on his new Sandwalk
he had a sense of sudden attack
& whirled around to catch
the imagined crouching creature at work,
brandishing his stick at the trees
then running ahead a little, heart thumping.

In his dreams Darwin heard sheep
screaming as the wolf
ripped them open, dragged entrails
over the clover
until one could not tell the difference
between the sweet pink heads
of the flowers & the speckle
of sheep guts dotting the grass.

The rest of the flock stayed huddled
for a day under the trees
as sparrows darted past,
though they kept chewing.

Habit

Muscles habituated to movement
he noted, make motion without thought,
so thoughts when thought
too often turn habitual, see
the involuntary kick of religion.

How to acquire the habit
of pondering, say
to ponder pondering itself
while circling the Sandwalk
with an iron-shod stick
once a day, five orbits each mid-day,
because to encircle thought
too tightly, he truly thought,
was to kill it.

Sometimes he tried skipping
across the stones
just to see
what would happen.

Brodie

Her black skirts only stop cracklin
& sighin
when she pits herself
into the wicker chair
lowerin slowly

her copper brew
sloshin the saucer.

Nobody to see if she sips that too
& is weesht for a bird song.

Her ain sweet pets, those wee bairns
were at play

it had been Dark & Dismall all day

but their mither's hands were streamin o'er her quick tune
as sun after rain thru open rooms

& the Bees were Beeing

& her hatted maister Darwin
crunchin doon for his pebbled turn
(she could hear 'im)

was suddenly bent

ever queerly
ever quietly

a glass attached
to a band on his head

on his knees on the path
ootside the summer hoose
where she sat.

Wit he did she didnae ken
& she hoped he'd nae be ill again
while her tea was hot.

Brodie peered, leanin too
over the window sill.

She dinnae dare move
while Darwin struck still
but he didn't flinch a limb
for many long minutes
& her neck was soon cramped
& her temper crabbit
for lull of noon.

He was squint thru the glass
over a pale movin cone
of sand ever rapt, spellbound
& spent

a crick hour there
with red ants.

It's a shame ye dinnae 'ave more to do
with yer time
she thought

but by mine
my Godd

ye never see
an ant in kip

how much I estame it

& settlin back in
no heed
she must & just did
finish her Tea.

Erasmus Darwin

lunar, libertine abolitionist
poet of primeval filaments
& grandfather on his father's side
in the shape of a tall old clock
in the hallway—
startled Charles awake.
Three a.m. by his chime.

His grandfather's fame
often woke him, his old voice
in his ear chiding, *my boy,*
you've not gotten there yet.

In his dream
Charles had been telling
this dead grandfather:
I do not think it wise
to teach the children to see
lizards frogs zoophytes & worms as disgusting
to keep children in the dark…

as the two of them peered, one-eyed
through the microscope
at some slippery, swimming, unshelled thing
writhing on a slice of glass.

To his children's eyes
the slides in his room
contained simply nothing,

but did one not have to begin, he asked,
with the smallest to find the largest within?

As with Hooke's *Micrographia:*
Or Some Physiological Descriptions of Minute Bodies Made
by Magnifying Glasses with Observations and Inquiries
        Thereupon, 1665,
dedicated, TO THE KING
which his grandfather once owned
& began with the head of a needle
& then proceeded
through every imaginable & complex thing
that could be fit
beneath a ground lens.

Or J. B. Robinet's *Philosophical Views*
On the Natural Graduation of Forms of Existence
or the attempts made by nature while learning
to create humanity, 1768,
in which the author suggested
that each fossil shell was a different
human organ
practicing shapes for later existence & man
was their progressive end point,
his body
just an assembly of shells.

Darwin had never met his philosopher grandfather
that famous Doctor (& infamous lover)

who'd chopped off his best friend's leg
without anaesthetic;

who believed that science could be clarified
like wine
through poetry & so wrote
every truth then known
about botany
in sensual book-long verse—
polygamous plants
of such promiscuous intercourse
that it had made
Charles's sixteen year old body burn;

& who painted three scallop shells, his coat of arms,
on the side of his carriage
(sped from patient to patient while inside he read)
blasphemously adding

e conchis omnia:
everything from shells.

Ink

The sea had made him
it was true
more expansive of mind
but evasive too,
jelly-like
able to dart
into the tiniest fissures
in the stones

but for a scrawl of chestnut ink.

When watched, he stayed motionless
awaiting his moment
colour-shifting, cloudy, chameleonic,
then he advanced by stealth
an inch or two
before shooting away
to safe hole
deeper waters.

Once fixed there
with suckers
only great forces
could unstick him.

How long had Charles felt
that fish shadow & sea had shaped him,

lured him like those wild men he'd met without stitch
to cover them, but stalked by animal
vapours, their cloth & totem.

He confessed it sleepily one night
his arm enwrapping the curve
of Em's hip, jelly-like, he thought,
in perfect plumpness
& those two forms fused:
the sponge of skin & ink seepage
from fingers that clasped her
life-dependent,
pouring out the two hundred & thirty-one secret pages
he would keep
hidden with boots & coats beneath the stairs
while his octopus-totem hovered
over their bed.

Was it science that bound them
fish & man
so tightly together?
Or 'selection by death'
(a hurricane thought
he'd have to note
in the morning)
& those he
selected to die?

He saw again how
after he'd snatched it from the water
the octopus had tried
to crawl away, unable to lift
its massive head from the sand.

Later, in the ship's pitch
in night's starred black fist
too violent for lantern or candle,
his steel nib scratched the dark.
His catch kept in the corner of his cabin,
glowing, glowering, phosphorescent,
hideous as sick.

For years, afterwards, whenever Emma found him shunting
around his study upon his black stool's caster wheels
grabbing for eight things at once, she'd call him
affectionately, her octopus.

Marriage

"Detective Darwin," his wife would muse
  as he sloshed in heavy-headed, mind-leaded from his room
"have you any extraordinary news, any vexing but enchanting clues
  for me? A new barnacle perhaps, a perplexing addition
  to your family tree we marine-wives at tea
  teasingly call your Monster & Co? Though we don't mind
  the slime of innuendo, or the wild surmising
  when you & your heretical friends
  (although I do like the chutney that Mr Hooker sends)
  preach undersea reproduction
  the stalks & sacks & budding of creatures;
  we do not mind Mr *Arthrobalanus*, your deviant little barnacle,
  nor the fact that you seem to be
  increasingly cirripede-like (I have noticed your whiskers
  waving at me), or even that you light your room
  with luminous zoophytes at night
  but I have been bothered by these strange constant leaks
  of saltwater under doors
  & do not speak of hermaphrodites
  & double penes &c &c over the soup please,
  at the very least when the children are present."

"Don't be cross at me dear wife & cousin Em, life is a contest
  of forces, a Hegelian joust. Let the strongest forms
  by their strength survive, & the weakest forms, well you see…
  & you, my sweet, are the perfect example
  of the emergence of beauty
  (though not order) from the struggle to be.

But I know you will wish me & my barnacles *al Diabolo*
when you hear of the half-inch female species, Mrs *Ibla*,
I found today, whose body, like a jacket, has two pockets
each manned by a tiny husband, & would you believe
what I do, that *'embedded in the flesh of their wives*
they pass their whole lives…as testis, mere bags of spermatozoa
& can never move again?' But I shan't say
a word more about it, will upset you, except that I sense
my truth is a virtue & these minute males are truly
wonderful. Evidence that my species theory
(like confessing a murder I know) is *gospel.*"

"It takes no quick work to know
that the wonder & riddle is one such as she,"
Emma said, "(the stronger sex indeed!)
who will put up with two useless, purple, sack-like chaps
affixed to her skirts & her bed for eternity without rest?
Asexual sprouting, or whatnot, no matter,
this cannot make for feminine happiness
with or without Heaven
but only proves as *gospel* what I, Emma,
dutiful and true, already knew:
that man & wife being constantly together for life
should have its limits.
Don't try to unseat me with your lance, dear Charley,
I have already budded seven for you."

After Breakfast

Darwin went to his dark room
to think.

He was testing success
in deceiving a headache
called this his metaphysical work.

Best method: let mind skip
from subject to subject,
let intensities shift.
The senses in sleep were like this.
His life he made like this.

'*Answered*,' he scrawls next to its question
in the margin of his notebook.

Writes: *Evolutionary thought*
as dangerous as social revolution,
eruptions. Earth's
crust, cities, creatures
in slow, constant flux.
Fixed forms eternal
was always Plato's fault.

Then, a great shout in the passageway outside his study
& the clatter of wood down the worn carpet
of the sliding staircase:
Annie head-first, or George eight steps standing,

they *banged*
the board into the wall of his room.
The wild yelp.

He couldn't see the need for separations for things
like wives & work
children & books
thought & sleep
Picus bones spread over the billiard green
Luccinea in coat pockets & he believed
that everybody would be insane
anyhow, eventually.

The trembling knock
on door, shy feet, weeping.
'Don't look, Papa, there's blood.'
A queasy red seep, hands searching drawers
through string, bones, litmus paper, four hundred barnacle
    boxes
for a sticking plaster.
He faces the window while Annie wraps
Etty's split finger.

He always lets the children in.
He likes to break his habits.

To prevent headache, no thought could be thought too deeply
but he'd learned to skim ideas like books,

questions only partially answered
while hopping over the eons
over the great gasps of time in the time
it takes him to reach his study door
& cross the sprouting branches of rooms
transmutated by children:
fortresses of blue satin sofa piled in the parlour.
Stepping across croquet mallets, shoes, forceps, pencils, mail
trails of orange peel, pocket magnifying glasses;
in the time it takes a child to become a man—
Francis standing sentinel duty in the corner
with bayonet for his father, not kiss—
past tools & fossil of tooth, stuffed finch & out

to where flashes of flax-flower blue shine through
the brim of his straw hat
like dreams
to which he has no answer.

She Played

pianoforte for him
when his hands trembled
from dissecting
too many luminous creatures aquatic
eyes flinching like filaments.
Microscopic tremors.

She played with the yellow lamp
on her left
casting light softer than moth
wings over her skin.

The plaintive tapping
of her satin slipper
her slim foot rising & falling
filled & calmed him.

How much more immediate
were the effects of music on his mind, his spine.

All throughout tea
he'd waited for this time.

Sometimes he watched her fingers
climb the chords, as though many-legged,
ravelling & unravelling clues
like Hume's witty, infinite spider
spinning the world from its bowels.

Sometimes she played Bach
with a parlour-pervading sadness
her face otherwise rarely possessed

but mostly she played Mozart
though not by heart.

Definitions for Happiness

A thick cotton shirt
across your back
dozing with a book in your lap,
tickling the children.

Picking wild pink sorrel
and dog-daisies for your wife,
musing on a stone
that seems a precious ancient bone,
dreaming of dinner and a strong
brown drink.

The hot drop into a morning's bath,
tracking bees beneath the hedges,
wondering where the flies go
when it rains.

Cracking a joke like a coconut.
Cracking ice puddles.
Cracking your back
after hunching over a table for too long.

A word of praise in the post
from a friend.
Hot buttered toast.
Another cup of tea.

Crossing paths with your wife
by the stairs at mid-day

where the wrought iron shadows
lay over the stone floor,
sharing how baby Lenny on lap said
Well you old ass...
and lingering there
in private laugh.

Two daughters as tall as the window sash
heaving heavy legs through the grass
passing your study window
on wooden stilts.

Remembering Tasmania.

Scraping your nails across
the cloth cover of a good book
of which you still have more
than half to read.
Your little son beating your back
in time to the piano.
Humming a Welsh tune.

Making traps of hazel twigs.
Spying a bird's nest full of pale blue eggs.
A child called Snow.

Eating gooseberries
alone.

The rain on the roof, the distant chatter
of children in bed in other rooms
who believe they are keeping quiet.

Clean sheets. Two pairs of bare feet
meeting
under the summer quilt.

Your daughter on the swing in the garden
singing.

The smell of ink
the sharp end of the pen
tuning the microscope lens
the moment something amorphous
comes into focus.

The sharp relief
of scissors
slicing the clean square newsprint
of a good review.

Staring out the window as fog enlaces the trees
the sad evening fog
almost as perfectly blue as you
as it encloses your house
in a ghost's coat and keeps you
reading by the fire for hours.

Doctor Gully's Extraordinary Water Cure Establishment

Aqueous Treatment.
Two guineas a week.

Tennyson hadn't told him
he wasn't allowed to bring books.

Or that he'd be dunked naked into hydropathic vats
sloshed in baths
& swaddled at dawn in cold, sodden white sheets

then simmered over the Spirit lamp
again bound in wet blankets, set to melt
the effects of excessive mental exertion

buff the agitated dyspeptic body
the endlessly digesting body
the overexcited nervous system
the way a large floe of ice polished the boulders
at the edge of the sea.

Emma had hauled the whole family
bag & baggage cross-country.

Though he'd snuck in the last
of his eight years of barnacles
& notebooks past the gates with him

they too were banished.
With French novels. Rich food.

All over the spa-village of Malvern
the invalid & wretched
were moistened, then poised
on rented donkeys, trundled over the hills
clutching sloshing tumblers of clear water,
their pale skin dripping
in the light.

Darwin wasn't allowed to eat
'anything good'
for two months
just meat or egg, plain toast
no butter, no snuff
no writing, no work.

Daily he was doused & drenched
in cold compress across belly, across back,
sunk in baths of ice water, scrubbed red-raw,
rough-towelled, waterfalled
in thunderous rush from pipes above.

Though indeed the water cure
momentarily broke the disease—
his doubts, his plague of secrets—
it dulled his brain. He was so numbed with cold
that when he woke at dawn he was
more amoeba than man
& it took several hours to become
fully human again.

After his morning's vomit
he would recall the delightful days
in fossil past
when one had only
a suckered, masticating mouth
& no such organ
as a stomach.

The Time Traveller

He often didn't know who or where he was
when he woke in dark places.
Was he proceeding to Bahia Blanca with men & *posta*
in the year 1833? Those slow, aching inches
on their horses across the deserted sandstone plain that day
past the last drying-up water holes, each puddle
clear but undrinkable. Twenty hours after salty meals
of kid goat & roasted armadillo in the shell
one poncho-ed Gaucho pointed
to the salt-encrusted ground where he would lay his head,
here we will sleep.
Darwin stirred, recalling thirst greater than ever
he'd known, as if he'd drunk all night the sea
& he gulped happily to the chin the jug of clean
cold water beside his English bed.

This time traveller
(he who lived his days in two times:
one geological, philosophical, everlasting;
the other, fast, insignificant, human days,
tasks, clocks, life-time)
suffered the displacement of hours,
the lapses of a body long
since adapted to passing through rock
slabs of geologic history
on which were etched eras, epochs, ages;
while others around him
simply stepped through a door into the parlour
hoping to get warm by the fire.

It took no small family work
to revive him from minutiae:
the retina of a fly, serratures of the bee,
the electric organs of fishes;
or to make him see with two human eyes & then tickle
the real, chattering, toothful, roving
animalcules of his household;
to shift him off the ever-shifting, ever-elusive
tectonic plates of mind
as though stepping off a carousel
onto stable ground to find yourself
still moving. For Charles, passing the plates around the table
often took on a whole new dimensional significance.
He'd watch the Wedgwood piled with potatoes go round:
a transportal of pebbles; or see the red shards of earthenware
he'd once found on San Lorenzo
on a plain high above the beach, in every
teacup the children dropped.

A whole day could elapse in a moment
between the taking of a cup of tea & stirring it;
or an epoch pass
while a man walked a circuit of the Sandwalk, the Earth
circling the sun millions of times in this time & fish
found their fins on land could be legs
& showed off
their new skill, unabashedly blinking & slinking past.

During the munching of luncheon beans,
the delicate squeaking
of green skins in his jaws, he'd think
lizard feeds on sea-weed—
but by then it would be morning again, a year later or two,
after a night where, as a magician of instance
he'd conjured a future that was already long gone
& he saw the trees fall, grow, fall again & cities bloom
as algae bloomed
& he discovered his wife, like an extinct Siberian beast, caught
under the ice. He clawed his nails to the blood-quick
smearing the snow with red to get to her—too slow—
he woke
abruptly, relieved, to feel her breathing, warm & still,
while all the birds outside his window cried
tempus fugit.

March, 1851

My Dearest Fox,

my daughter and I
have twin influenzas.

I lie all day on the sofa
with *Phases of Faith*.
She clings & cries upstairs.
No longer combs
my hair.

How strange to feel
one's child's pulse beat feeble. I fear
she has inherited
my condition. Trouble with children
is you love them so.

We are off again to Dr. Gully
for the steaming. He will cure her
if anyone can.

Call the Black Horses

– Annie Darwin, 1841–1851

Open the room to let in more air,
let the late April light cast a new path
across the shadows.
Your pen today carries too much ink,
the vital force it drips depletes
all thunder mute. You cannot speak.

Last night she tried to sing. By noon
human things weighed too much
in passing, hurt too much, sharp
grain of days inching through veins
through the guts like sand,
a pile of hard seeds you'll never digest
in your hand.

Call the black horses, pluck the ostrich plumes.
Make an altar in the yew, after the famed one
whose empty winter branches
held tufts of thread, bread, meat, hat and crepe.
Match colours to their matter
to see her black-grey eyes again.
Attach backs of nut-hatch, flint, Hawthorn stems.

You can safely put God to bed now
the way you can't your daughter anymore.
Tuck the sheets so tight he cannot move
and lock the bedroom door.

Heaven for Women

In ominous thunder death came hounding Down.
The hard black rain bombarded the roof, the stark
trunks of trees were doused in sudden lightning
candles fluttered in the draught & no book
he found eased the doubt
& every bit of every thing brought dread—
wet wind over the window ledge,
dark spots before his eyes made him think
he was dying, & the children
shivered on the bed.

Emma said there's nothing in thunder
to fear. God's moving
his table & chairs around Heaven.
Charles frowned for what she claimed
as so easily known, as her own.

Yet into the unknown he went daily
while the cold jolt to the spine he felt
at the idea of the loss of his existence
knocked him sideways.
The Gospel of John would not cure him now
nor Coleridge's emotional innate faith
which could not be innate if not felt, could it? Even fear
of eternal burning would not warm him.

He'd long noted the irony
that those with strength in Scripture
pledged to ignorance, passed in peace;
while those who vowed to know
that which would otherwise remain
unknown, writhed with fear.

Irrational belief may strike out
the dizzy spell at the loss of conscious self
but if their Heaven be full of the blind
certainty they call faith, a library
with only one book in it,
he wouldn't be stuck there a day, much less
an eternity.

As he left the room, Henrietta asked Emma
where was the Heaven for women
because all the angels in the pictures
were men?

– V –

"How awfully flat I should feel, if when I get
my book together on species &c &c, the whole
thing explodes like an empty puff-ball.—"

– C.D. to Joseph Hooker, 1854

To be a Seed

Late at night he imagined the dispersal of seeds
across seas, could imagine the distances
in the instance of finches
strewn by wind and wing
but how did those fragile seeds swim?
Were they carried in the guts of ducks
or trapped like bubbles in an ice floe
floating until slow snow melt released them?
Did they hook like barnacles to the wood of rafts?
And what of plants? And what of snake eggs
wholly floating, bobbing the waves
to new places? And once there, and once born,
once cracked open,
how did one live on entirely foreign islands?
By wits? By chance? By sheer
stubborn determination
to be?

To be a seed.

To survive the tilted, pitched mystery
of your own ship;
to endure 1400 miles of saline drift
and then, beached
bury yourself into the dirty cleft of hollow driftwood
on the damp base of a island cliff—
was this the sheer will
that began it all?

And what was the life
of the newest exile like
before it found a mode and a habit
a transmutable plasticity
that let it gaze upon this puddle of water, this mud-hole
this strange insect, not quite like
the puddles, the mud-holes or the insects of its homeland and kin
but not wholly unlike or unkind either
and think, well, alright,
I'll give it a try?

Those that do not try
die.

                    *

The bead of life immersed
in salt-water for forty days and forty nights
when planted, still cracks
open, pours forth
its small green life, its shootable, edible tendril,
its fingerprint of possibility.

Seeds packed in the basement in jars of snow.
Seeds floating in bowls in the kitchen cupboard
like spirits he might drink in order to know
how much to make the vital force expire?
How to force the end
in ten easy steps? Or will they grow?

These seeds he stashed, and tried
in pottering Squire's experiments
to kill a dozen ways:
to drown, freeze, smother, swallow and crush
then planted in glass dishes,
he watched bloom, despite all sense.

For to 'untie the knot' and prove
his doctrine: life's chance battle,
he had to show how and why it died.
Yet he found, again and again
that it so wanted to live.

In the Kitchen

Cut up that pig's head
those tough little trotters
chop off the ears, tongue & cheeks.
Slice 6 lbs of lean meat
& pickle for a week.

Light the wood
heft the stew pot
mix sugar, vinegar
to this brew.

Boil the head & stir
till meat slips from the bones.
Add 6 onions, 2 carrots, turnips
savoury herbs.

Take the pork out
& pound it into shape.
Boil again for an hour,
put on a weight
til it is pressed
new loaf of head
on a plate.

Then send it
cold and direct
to the table.

In the Study

For pigeons, try chloroform
or a bath of arsenic soap might do.
Boil them in a large pot
no less than twelve minutes
by the watch.

Stir stew of potash
silver oxide
jam down the rotting flesh.

Slay & skeletonise
the sweet Fan-tail chicks
the white Angora rabbits;
tie up the wings
of large birds
with string.

Slit, hang & flush
& tip the boiling water in.

Lay skins in boxes
soaked in turpentine.
Mix equal parts
water & wine
for all but crabs
who prefer
their pickling neat.

The Tiniest Things

When they were ill
they were let into his study
to lie still under the window
& watch him tussle
with the world's tiniest things;
his script they couldn't fathom
nor the slippery shrimp
springing out of his hands,
scuttling across the floor
like commas.

Scallop shells
when scalpeled
contained prizes so small
there was nothing at all
but alphabet letters it seemed—
the pearl of an 'o' maybe,
the grit of a 't'.
Letters from the post
when sliced open often spilled out
three feathers
from goose tails
were bedtime stories or quills
hollow, black-inked, sharp-bladed;
they were sad
(as Bull-dog puppies soaked in salt)
when plucked from live ducks.

Pouter pigeon chicks
kept in the outside aviary were too soon
boiled in potash stink
for skeletonising. Inside their house

corpses
everywhere.

Chance & Necessity, 1858

"The varieties of man may seem to act on each other;
in the same way as different species of animals
the stronger always exterminating the weaker."
                    – C.D., The Voyage of the H.M.S Beagle

All the long June day the house was quiet
but for the constant tread
down the hallways, up the stairs
to still the sound of an infant coughing.

The news of an epidemic had spread
as quickly as the flush
of red on a child's face; three children in the village
already taken by the fever, the strawberry tongue.

Around him, pacing & packing
as his children were hustled out of the house to Sussex
while his namesake flailed in his cot.

The essay from a man named Wallace had come a week ago:
'On the tendency of varieties to depart infinitely
from the original type'. It threatened to obliterate
his half-finished book, twenty years of work & priority
but he was worn out now with worry
& left matters of trumpery
with his friends Hooker & Lyell to decide.

Chance & necessity
were two sides
of the struggle for existence
but what was the chance of two men
evolving the same theory
as Natural Selection
on separate sides of the planet?

He believed that nothing was immutable
nor placed in whole finished perfection upon this Earth.
Indeed, he could see around him
the way his loved ones fell.

Outside, the bees sucked flowers
shifting white pollen from pistils
beneath their abdomens
to their yellow fur before they flew away,
while the body of Charles Waring was taken away.

So he would take a chance on chance
& in necessity he would publish

or anon
he, too, would be.

The Stories

At the end of every scientific day

she gently led him from his labyrinth
into a novel way of thinking—

her throat pouring forth the stories
her fingers paging the yellowbacks
her voice a ribbon of light

& he wondered
if more clarity lay in her fictions,
in the simplicity of their beginnings, middles & ends
than in his endless empirical plodding.

Trying to make sense of pigeons
ten papers cross-referencing
ten books without as much as a look upwards,
philosophical riddles rioting
accumulating details like middens:
seeds in owl pellets, dead land-birds in sea-drift
nature would not do as he wished,
the laws of each species
still out of reach.

He struggled to put his own words together
struggled with the stone-heft of facts;
struggled to have a story as clear as that
which Emma told him.

Mrs D

patiently nursed his illness
marked the days
in her diary
'poorly', 'great lethargy'
'much improved'
as if it were her own
body's churn & fevers
she charted.

She ordered ever more
complicated
varieties of pudding to serve
his strange stomach
though often
he could only eat rice.

Mrs Grice in the village
dispatched recipes for bread rolls
& skim milk pudding & white
sauce. 'How *is* your husband's
indigestion?' she'd imprudently ask
before launching into long
tracts of advice
where everything depended
'on the yeast being good.'

Emma was pregnant again
confined to her ballooning
pigeon body, her bedroom,

to her tenth nine-months of pain.
Charles claimed to feel it, feel
each as keenly as she
though he neatly administered
the chloroform over her nose
when she called for it
& tried to stay standing
until the doctor came.

Some mornings they both
spent in swoon, bent
vomiting over porcelain bowls.
Man & Wife, she'd later muse,
so worn she waddled
past his sofa bed

two species
united by nausea.

Symptoms, Cures

The first time he ever saw him, the famous naturalist,
he was hunched over, half-crushed with pain,
dragging his withered physiognomy
through the door of his Moor Park rooms.

Dr Lane sighted a great white & half-
balding head, tiny eyes shrunk & deep-set
from too much peering out. These were overhung
by a beetling *appendicium* of bone
that held in place the weighty toppling brain,
still throwing out sparks,
which the body could no longer hold up.

The young man peered down at the old man
aged well beyond his forty-eight years.

"Symptoms?"

"Dizziness, eczema, flatulence, gout, headaches, lethargy,
 boils & sores, swellings, strange twitching, fainting, black
         spots, & vomiting
 after every meal & several times as well nightly, for years."

"Cures?"

"Amyl nitrate, arsenic, batteries, bismuth, diets,
 Indian Ale, hydropathy, Spirit lamps,
 ice bags on the lower back,
 sucking whole lemons, sipping acid concoctions

to strengthen gastric juices, *Condy's Ozonized Water Cure*,
electric chains doused in vinegar,
wires of zinc & brass looped around waist & neck
& rubbing tartar emetic ointment on my stomach."

Darwin shrugged,
"*No hay remedio*, as they say
in South America. I'm giving way
to the way of nature."

The Slave

Wearing brass chains around his wrists
& neck for his pain, Charles recalled
the South American slaves he'd once seen
& wanted so badly to free. And yet
he still wore these, willingly. He claimed
again & again to doctors, to all who knew him
his stomach was the culprit
but he wondered in truth if it was what he knew
that was to blame. His brain,
his need to pry free
the whole skull from the dumb rocks
to shout, break chains—
versus his need for praise
for quiet habitation, routine
among the slow, calm of silent, insensate things.

"You see, I have been most preoccupied of late
with my Species Book.
Slow work, my life's work. I hope
I live
to finish it."

Dr Lane prodded his stomach
with cold fingers,
held up the vial of urine
to the light.

Gorilla

It had been *gorillas this, gorillas that*
for ages.

Across the continents
bidding wars
for gorilla bones.

Gorilla Quadrille For Piano
flew off the shelves.

Fashionable London ladies
swarmed to places
where naturalists were prominent
in the hopes of seeing a 'dear gorilla.'

The Americans had beaten the British to publication,
a taxonomic classification of what Owen named
Gorilla gorilla gorilla
as if its repetition
could prove more resolutely
the distinctness of its species.

When Wombwell's Travelling Menagerie
finally came, bearing a live gorilla

a black-skinned, high-bottomed brethren
grasping for contact through the bars of her cage,
the crowds pushed in
to gawk & rattle the cold metal

& watch her live eyes gawk back
as she rattled the length of her small new life
& back again.

The people were proud of the Power of their Nation
to conquer, catch, & hold
but were all relieved when she finally closed those eyes & slept
sitting with her head inclined forward on her breast,
snoring a little. The children stomped
threw peanuts to wake her, dared each other
to step closer until she caught
a perfect English cold, a rasping cough
that made her sound
as though she were drowning;
a husky-throated mute trying to speak
a single word before drowning,
then sticky, filling
wet-lunged pneumonia.

She was soon stuffed by Waterton.
He created a strange assemblage of skins
to form a horned simian sculpture he called
Martin Luther After His Fall.

Lost

Mostly, he slept certain.
On his back, in a straight line,
his life and spine more firmly formed
by years at sea than by
his wife. Though occasionally

she'd feel him curl around her
and murmur *mmmm-hmmm* as if
in mid-conversation upon some long-
pondered thought
that had been absorbing his mind
since morning.

She'd lie awake in night's creak
check the children's sleep,
then she'd creep down to the kitchen
to turn the salting pig.
Afterwards, she'd slip into the dark
room at the bottom of the stairs
where he sat each day
measuring the weights of animal bones
upon a postal scale.

Doubt did not follow him there.

She'd touch the tools he used: the tiny
silver knives, spools of cotton thread
stolen from her work basket, pill boxes
filled with black beetles, & the old rough

barnacles bent like her hands
already aching with the rain.
She did not touch his pages.

Sometimes there the hours took her.
Immeasurable time.
She'd sit by his window & hold
a bright white bird's skull
the size of a walnut
in her palm
until she warmed it.

Soon, the larks in the trees beyond the lawn would begin to call.

She did not call it prayer.
She called to her lost children
beneath the ground.

The Orchis Bank

Though he hadn't spoken of her out loud
for years, he'd never forgotten her.
And now, here, saw her again
with some shame as he paused his wet pen
over his pages, amendments
for the second edition of his great work.
Only a month out, but already he'd been swayed
into an act of self-transmutation
by the contradictions
the stubbornly vocal, blind faith
of other men.

He couldn't speak her name, and he tried
to pretend he couldn't see her watching him
as his nib scraped the paper, screeched the air,
left dry, thin scratches, unseemly blotches.

'There is grandeur in this view of life, with its several powers,
having been originally breathed into a few forms or into one...'

While he felt sure there were some
who'd been cross as thunder when they found
that each bolt of lightning, otherwise caused,
had not been forged by the hand of God alone—
he'd held the black tubes left in the dunes of Maldonado
from so forceful a strike they fused the sand to glass—
or that the length of the Earth's days
were not measured by the needs of men's sleep,

he did not want
to be the sole spoiler of their Sunday week.

He was not surprised to find the pain that accompanied
        publication
could be perfectly mapped as it acted upon his body
like bold bolts of lightning, like a child's death;
nor that The Times' cartoons would put him off his food.
Though he privately cursed The Ways
of Reviewers, the torturous wait
for views, he was too easily wounded.

'There is a grandeur in this view of life,
with its several powers, having been originally breathed
by the Creator into a few forms or into one...'

Annie down on the carpet
poised seal-like on elbows, as she compared
(as was her way) word for word any two
editions of any book, was a distant chirp in his ear:
"Papa why does it here say 'by the Creator'
and here not?" She had not missed
his sleight of hand.

If only he could tell her how
he remembered best the orchis bank,
his children's determined collection of the plants
beside him; now a kind of mnemonic place,

as he could not step onto the Sandwalk without seeing her
spinning her pirouettes before him in the sand.
So this paragraph, the last paragraph in his book
was not just a final flourish
of hard-won rhetoric, the grand trumping of argument
even thus amended, but expressed
the most deeply felt feeling:
from so simple a beginning
how much had he done and seen.
And she was but one of the *endless forms*
most beautiful and most wonderful
he meant, evolved now as the worms that fed
inside the open mouths of long-gone birds,
so Annie lived there, in his last words.

– VI –

"*I am a withered leaf for
every subject except Science.*"

– C.D., 1868

Julia Margaret Cameron
framed the old man

with his back to the window
at Freshwater Bay

made him remove
his slouch hat, his black cloak,
placed his head in the iron brace.

The hot sun sketched the line
of his suit coat, his button-holes
made each white hair
of his long beard glow

while in the dark she coated
countless wet plates
in collodion & silver nitrate

then lifted the lens lid
& exposed the glass to him
for seven minutes.

We both
take something unknown
& bring it closer
don't you think?
She asked.

I moved, I think, Darwin said.

She dunked his face
into the cyanide bath
fixing him there.

Lesson

He'd taken Bernard onto his knee
to explain the basics of evolution
beginning with Jenny, the Ourang-Outang
who howled like a child for apples
and wore clothes to meet the Queen
and continuing on backwards from there
or forwards, as you will,
genealogies, consanguinities,
wings, hands, flippers,
time, time, time.
His five-year-old grandson was wide-eyed
throughout the tale of tails
then without further word
quickly nipped away.

This was the first time
this particular story was told
and he was the first
grandfather or father to do so, but
he would not be the last.

Darwin later overheard Bernard
explaining to his nursemaid
that he'd once been an ape
before he became a big boy.

And that evening he caught him
studying his milky arms

in the garden, his stubby little hands,
head bent back, staring up
into the trees.

Repeat Lesson

Though he'd set aside the time
to again explain from the very beginning,
making sure the child understood
that Time was longer than any of their lives
and longer even than all of mankind
mankind's descent and all
of its slow metamorphic
steps along the way,

Bernard still came to him one day
shaking, clutching a thin newspaper clipping
he'd found stashed
between the pages of a book:

Darwin, grey-bearded, black-furred, hunched
with claws and paws clutching branches
ready to spring.

A Venerable Ourang-outang
A Contribution to Unnatural History

the caption beneath
the cartoon read

and the child cried
because his Grandfather had
after all, lied.

A Family Attempts to Rouse the Worms

They took to getting up in the dark
in order to flash candle & lamp-light
into the dirt-filled glass pots.

Only the brightest, a tiny lighthouse beam
sweeping across their nocturnal writhing secrets
could startle them, send them scarpering
rabbit-like, back to their burrows.

The pots were then set on top of the piano
while Emma played a stirring march
then a melancholy one
to see if they responded to sadness.
Their pale pink Earth-casting bodies
continued casting forth small spirals of dirt
but were no more moved by Handel's
The Arrival of the Queen of Sheba from Solomon
than by Chopin's *Nocturnes*.

They did not even stir at the low
pitch addition of Frank's bassoon
Bernard's little tin whistle
or Bessy's own shouts & yowling.

And while his grandfather took copious notes—
noting preferences for carrots over cabbages
with celery falling somewhere in between;
or how the worms, blind, deaf,
senseless as they seemed, had their own heightened sense

of what was right, the wriggling pleasure
of two worm bodies enjoined
was enough for worms to seek it out
even in the dread of light—

the best sense roused in that room
was the joy a family felt
hopping & tooting long past bedtime.

His grandfather's face, his love
when he grinned at him
he'd never forget
the night they tried to rouse the worms.

The Movements and Habits of Truth

Science was a game of truth he played
without a stacked hand;
not simple discovery
something carried from fossil light
out into the glare of a tropical sun to be seen
but a unit of reasoning that demanded
propagation, coral branching,
the mad sprouting of Chiloé's apple trees,
a whole wood being born from one tree
that enveloped the previous view
& the entire town, so,
no truth
without a culture to cut & cultivate it.

Still, he flushed it out
like a bird from the brush.

He was delicately pollinating
truth with his paintbrush
scattering hopeful wildflower seeds
in search of brave change.

Truth was a tendril that curled
towards the light
a clemantis hook that could clamp
onto anything in its path.

Mostly, truth, he knew
was a matter of fluency, a great speech
at the podium in a flood-rush of perfect expression,
though sadly, only as sound
as a civilization's plumbing
whether it then stops
or flows on.

The Death of the Transmutationist

In the dream
he was to be hung.
It was that simple.

The high wooden platform
on Castle Hill
with its circle of rough rope
was surrounded
by concentric circles of species and types,
a target practice of old classifications
with Darwin the archer's heart.
Beginning from there with the Cambridge
Dons and clergy, all the old guard who'd come
to see him fall (it was his fault
they weren't sleeping well),
and continuing on
through the atheists, rogues, dissenters
and the women,
followed by the mammals
the birds, the fish, and then
at the very back
scrambling to get a look
by perching on the shoulder of a kind iguana
were the barnacles and limpets.

The Blasphemous Transmutationist
in the Era of Creation
was asked to speak.

He turned around and raised
his hairline, showed
the long red scar where
he'd already been decapitated.
He cracked jokes about his hero's wounds
won for the good fight and twenty
years of stomach cramps. He spoke
eloquently, finally,
about the dangers of arrogant Man.

Only the animals at the back
clapped.

They had come out in support
of the fossil resurrectionist
who alone
seemed to see
how they felt
about their slavery
and how they too experienced
'*fear, pain, sorrow
for the dead*' and also the very, very
soon-to-be dead.

The hangman offered Darwin
a handful of nuts, but when,
he reached for them, Darwin saw
the pores in his hands
were bursting with black fur.

The man snatched the nuts away
before he could touch them,
then pulled the lever
and dropped the floor.

Darwin watched the animals
in the distance
contort in grimace, sulk and torment
then remember their indifference
as he twitched
from the noose.

Even then
his fingers were itching
to write.

– VII –

"*I have awakened in the night.
being slightly unwell & felt so much afraid…*"

– C.D., 'M' Notebook

The Last Notebook

Have children ideas of time?
Do monkeys cry?

Have you solved it yet?

His grandson hops the steps
without counting them
& does not watch the hands
on the clock go round. It is slow
Darwin notes, in the end,
the way life drips out the sides,
trickles along the edges of the self,
spills like saliva across the corner of the mouth
& as he hobbles around the Sandwalk one afternoon,
counting each step, clutching a thought
on the mental merits of worms
& their unrecognised contribution to the history of the world,
he drops down suddenly

The Green Need, April, 1882

The fear comes.
It is stronger than pain.
It is stronger than regret.

It worms its way through all
I could not say
all these years
to you
on the subject of death's
untouchable mystery;
the true question at the heart
of all this fumbling
the burning heaving heart
of the Earth, the rising crust,
the trajectories of animal time
and the sky's cold black distance

and how none of these truths
mean anything next to
the truth of you.
Hard won.
Soon lost.

*

Why does death
not grow easier
over time?

Is suffering compatible
with the battle itself?
Why is life short?
Why have we not adapted
to pain? Our modifications
of mind, matter, mass,
seem piecemeal, chancy, like half-forgotten
limbs, or stunted organs we cannot jettison
nor use, nor pass onto our children
though beautiful in their own way
for their imperfections;
the leafy tendril of vine that will still
reach out
of itself to clasp
something, anything,
the way it inches forward and wraps its whole body
so tightly
around a dead tree—
oh, the green need
to be.

Or the moth that flings itself
into its three days of life
with no defensive thought, nor regret
for the shortness of its breath
in the moment its wings hit
the candle's gold blaze.

How I envy at times
the blind faith of its being,
its sure arrow into the flame.
Surely the fire's danger
to the survival of moth should mean
life-protective revision, and yet
again and again, moths
hurl themselves
into the burning.

Is it better to know in advance
this is the only chance we get?
Is it better to know
not vague probabilities, but
what will happen
exactly and how it will feel
in the end?
How much better I can
hold your hand then.
My body will be earthworm
and you, my darling
will be far away
in your vast Heaven.
Never will we be
so far apart.

But late at night the rat's scratch
comes, this fear that I am wrong.
In the twelfth hour of the last day
I am wrong. Not in my calculation
of time's true logistics, but that
in my endless pursuit of the mystery
of mysteries, perhaps, I forgot,
perhaps I did not realise
that only in mystery
can we bear the pain.

Though Montaigne said
we fear pain
for the death it brings, not death
for its pain,

I'd think again
about that equation. Perhaps not
even death, not even pain.
We fear *fear*
for it alone is boundless.

Will you hold me, now, like this?
Will you ever hold me as you hold me today?
Your arms so strong, your love
most fierce with unwavering, rising belief.

Will you let me weep
for the salvation of our last moments?
As you wipe my vomit, blood from my beard, my cold sweat,
as you kiss my head and clasp
tightly my trembling limbs to your limbs
I am
in the end just a body
bursting
out of its love.

Afterwards

the house felt empty.
Though she was more aware
than ever
of the rustling
of life beneath the roof and eaves
the mice and birds
felt safe
to come out again.

She read out loud to herself
on the couch, continued the novel
where they'd left off, turning
the tiny gold ring around her finger,
heaved his old books
onto her lap.

Hume's *Dialogues Concerning Natural Religion*
lasted but a night.

She took up his cigarette
once, foolishly,
choked on the bitter smoke
as grey ash scattered
over the blue satin.

She played backgammon
moving one piece
then another, playing for him,
remembering his raucous admonishment

(*"Bag your bones!"*) when she beat him
and the click
of the worn marble circles
like cold stones in her hand.

She clipped the fascinating
crime stories, the curious trials
from *The Times*, tried to predict
in advance from the facts, as he'd done,
who'd done it.

When it was late
she climbed the stairs
and sometimes
looked back quickly,
hoping to glimpse him
shuffling out of his study
one last time
to pinch a bit of snuff

bending
and unbending
his mind.

Emma

Years later
Darwin would come to the door
of the drawing room to see
if the clocks
moved any more quickly in there
than in his study.

She'd look up from the piano
his soft kind wife
her hands as a girl hand-curled by Chopin
& comment that either way,
that clock kept good pulse
for her music.

And stepping in,
& by the sight of a glinting rock
in the window sill's sunlight
behind her, he would be transported
back to that day in Australia
when he followed the glint
of creek-water to its end. How young
he had been then, dreaming
of Lyell's *Principles of Geology*
& hoping to write
a great work of his own.

And though his wife bemoaned
his loss of God

(he always believed
it was more like keys misplaced
at first mistakenly, though over time
un-replaced, once he learned
that doors left unlocked
& coats half-buttoned
let wayward, useful thoughts
like scarves of wind
slip in) he knew
he was not indifferent.

What other man
by their sick bed could mind
for hours in the window
the twining habits of vines
twirling to the left, twirling to the right
& barely finishing his cup of tea
record each spurt & curl
so dutifully?

He and Em had lived for years
in a mutual adaptation
as she entwined around the spine of family.
He had never stopped
loving her fingers
like little bolts of light
on the piano keys
or the tiny soft brown dot over her top lip.

Had she thought he hadn't noticed?
He who examined closely all things,
bent to a leaf or worm, one knee in the dirt,
one eye to the glass, magnifying the beauty?

Still, she would outlive him.
Her music, too.

And he would think of that creek & how all he knew
of marriage, of love
was embryonic then inside him;
now enlarged, a glint of light
he followed to the end
of his life, ducking
through the brush and branching
of water to find, either way,
how flimsy we are inside all of this time
really, how ephemeral.

"*If I had to live my life again I would have made a rule to read some poetry and listen to some music at least once every week; for perhaps parts of my brain now atrophied could thus have been kept active through use. The loss of these tastes is a loss of happiness and may possibly be injurious to the intellect, and more probably to the moral character, by enfeebling the emotional part of our nature.*"

– THE AUTOBIOGRAPHY OF CHARLES DARWIN

Some notes on the text

If one were to use only the material that Charles Darwin himself recorded about his life, it would be possible to write a dozen collections of poems. This book, therefore, necessarily represents only a fraction of Darwin's life, as told from my own perspective. It is poetry inspired by his life, a portrait of Darwin, but it is not a biography and any factual errors (or misconstruing) within it are my own.

I have quoted or been inspired by Charles Darwin's correspondence, writings, personal journals and notebooks in these poems. There is no consistent rhyme or reason but my own aesthetic and whim to the way I represent quotations within the book. Some are in italics; some are in quotes. When portions of the text are in both quotations and italics, it signals handwriting; as a way of visually representing Darwin's (or another's) writings. However, italics without quotation marks are also used to signal 'notebook jottings' that are not Darwin's words, but my own. At other times (just to confuse things), certain quotes are reproduced neither in italics nor in quotation marks, because of the way those markings affected the visual aesthetics of the poem. To help clarify what is mine and what is Darwin's, all of Darwin's actual words are cited below in the endnotes in their original forms. Anything else you can presume is my own rendering.

Many of Charles Darwin's notebooks and manuscripts can be viewed and read online (often in both original hand and transcribed) at Charles Darwin Online (www.darwin-online.org.uk), although nothing quite replaces the experience of holding his notebooks in your hand, trying to decipher his writing with a magnifying glass!

Charles Darwin also wrote and received thousands of letters in his lifetime. Approximately 14,500 of them are available online, most fully transcribed and wonderfully annotated, a passionate undertaking of the Darwin Correspondence Project team at Cambridge University (and then published in conjunction with Cambridge University Press): www.darwinproject.ac.uk

Darwin occasionally used strange spellings of familiar place names in his notebooks, such as Chiloe (or sometimes Chiloé), Buenos Ayres or Aires. I have retained these.

The village of Down, in Kent, that Charles and Emma moved to in 1842 was changed to Downe in 1850. Their house was, and continues to be, known as Down House. I have used the original spelling of Down in the poems to prevent any confusion.

Abbreviations for citations:
CCLC – Christ's College Library Cambridge
CD – Charles Darwin
CUL – Cambridge University Library
BL – British Library
EH – English Heritage (Down House, Kent)

Quotations from the Charles Darwin manuscripts and letters are by permission of the Syndics of Cambridge University Library.

Epigraph
"Poetry is not ..." The Full quote: "Poetry is not the proper antithesis to prose, but to science. Poetry is opposed to science, and prose to metre. The proper and immediate object of science is the acquirement, or communication, of truth; the proper and immediate object of poetry is the communication of immediate pleasure." Samuel Taylor Coleridge, *Definitions of Poetry* (1811), though Coleridge made this pronouncement while in the midst of a full-fledged opium habit, so I haven't taken it too seriously.

– I –

"I seem to remember him gently touching any flower he delighted in. This sounds sentimental but is was the same simple admiration a child might have. It ran through all his relations to natural things—a most keen feeling of their aliveness." Preliminary draft, Francis Darwin, 1884. 'Reminiscences of my Father's Everyday Life': CUL MS.DAR.140.3.1-159.

The Donkey, August, 1817

Charles Robert Darwin was born on 12 February 1809 in Shrewsbury, Shropshire, England, to Robert (a wealthy doctor) and Susannah Darwin (neé Wedgwood).

Charles's mother Susannah died of a tumour, in July 1817, when he was eight. His three older sisters, Catherine, Caroline and Susan, then helped his father to raise him.

The Plums

Charles's mother Susanna was the daughter of Josiah Wedgwood, the potter and manufacturer of Wedgwood china. Josiah was a good friend of Charles's grandfather, the poet and doctor Erasmus Darwin. When Charles himself decided to get married, he proposed to his cousin Emma Wedgwood.

June, 1828

"My dear Fox, I am dying by inches, from not having any body to talk to about insects." Extract from a letter of CD to his cousin William Darwin Fox, 12 June 1828: CCLC Fox 1. By kind permission of the Master and Fellows, Christ's College, Cambridge.

Sappho

Darwin had a little pointer called Sappho that followed him around Cambridge University one year. He began his first term at Cambridge in 1828. He took his degree in May 1831.

The Very Last Meeting of the Glutton Club

The dinner club of Cambridge friends was also called the *Gourmet*; CUL MS.DAR.112:113v-114.

'unknown to human palate", Frederick Watkins to CD, 18 September 1831: CUL MS.DAR.204:67.

In the Old Library

Both the poet John Milton (whom students referred to as 'The Lady of Christ's') and CD were students at Christ's College, Cambridge. Charles's rooms at Christ's had also previously been used by the Reverend William

Paley, whose texts *The Evidences of Christianity* and *The Principles of Moral and Political Philosophy* were required reading for Darwin's exams. When I say Charles was 'Paleyfied', I mean the unquestioning and expected acceptance the young Darwin had towards Paley's argument that the natural world, by its very creative diversity, infers a Creator, much like today's 'intelligent design' arguments.

Darwin carried a pocket edition of Milton's *Paradise Lost* with him on the *Beagle* voyage.

Venus

Darwin used to go to the Fitzwilliam Museum in Cambridge with his cousin William Darwin Fox and also with his brother Erasmus to behold Titian's *Venus* [*Venus Crowned by Cupid with a Lute Player*]. At the time, the painting was kept behind curtains due to its risqué depiction of nudity.

Burn This!—

Title taken from the postscript of one of Fanny Owen's letters to CD late January 1828: CUL MS.DAR.204:43.

"So I suppose I must trust to fate for a master or wait till you come.": Fanny Owen to CD, 9 March 9 1828: CUL MS.DAR 204:44.

In her letters, Fanny referred to Charles as 'dr Postillion' and herself as 'Housemaid', see various Fanny Owen to CD, i.e. late January. 1828: CUL MS.DAR.204:43.

"I've been so busy...*mania* go?': this is inspired by Fanny's letter to Charles when their relationship was cooling, but is not a word-for-word rendition. "I never *could* and never *shall* write like a lady"; "The *Duns* begin to ride—and the *King's Bench*—stares me in *the face*." See Fanny Owen to CD 27 January 1830: CUL MS.DAR.204:47.

"Burn this as soon as read—or tremble with my fury and revenge—"; "Red Coats and Moustachios": Fanny Owen to CD late January 1828 from Brighton: CUL MS.DAR.204:43.

Fanny and her sister called eligible young men 'Hares', as well as 'halterable' ['halter' for 'altar'] and 'shootable' and wrote "it is such exquisite fun galloping on the Downs as hard as one can go." See Fanny Owen to CD January 1828: CUL MS.DAR.204:42.

"utmost ar mony" Susan Owen (Fanny's sister) to CD 18 February 1828: CUL MS.DAR.204:59.

Fanny Owen married Robert Myddelton Biddulph in 1832 while Darwin was away on the *Beagle*. The marriage was reportedly unhappy with Fanny ending up cooped up in a Welsh castle.

The Beach
Prior to attending Cambridge, sixteen-year old Charles enrolled in Edinburgh University to study medicine (1825). He was horrified both by watching patients being operated on without anaesthetic and by the sight of blood. He was drawn more to the sea life found on Edinburgh's shores than to his anatomy classes. (Though the midwifery class he attended in 1826 would come in handy in later years – his wife had ten children.) He left Edinburgh after two years, without a degree.

– II –

This quote is adapted from a couple of different letters in which Darwin instructs his family to pack his things for his voyage on the *Beagle*. "Tell Nancy to make me 12 instead of 8 shirts..." CD to Susan Darwin, 6 September 1831: CUL MS.DAR.223:4; "Have my shirts marked DARWIN" CD to Susan Darwin, 17 September 1831: CUL DAR.MS.223:7.

Dearest Charley
Darwin's sisters often called him 'Charley'.

"...it will end by your wasting the best years of your life on ship board." Letter to CD from his sister Caroline Darwin written while Charles was on board the *Beagle*, 30 March 30 1835: CUL MS.DAR.97: B20-1.

Plunge
Count Alessandro Volta (1745–1827), physicist and inventor of the first electric battery.

The Vanishing
'bare living on blue water' CD to Caroline Darwin, [2] & 5 & 6 April 1832: CUL MS.DAR.223:10.

In a letter to his father Robert, Darwin describes the Sailor's ritual of being shaved when crossing the Equator, using tar and paint as shaving cream and a saw as a razor. He also praises the flowers, Cocoa Nuts, orange oranges and delightful beauty of the tropics: 8 & 26 February & 1 March 1832 CUL MS.DAR.223:8.

"It was impossible to behold this plain of matter as it were melted by heat, without being reminded of Milton's description of the regions of Chaos & Anarchy—" CD 24 October 1832, Bahia Blanca, heading towards Montevideo. *Beagle Diary* (1831–1836): EH 88202366. The original is kept at Down House, the property of English Heritage.

Diodon: porcupinefishes or balloonfishes. "— When handled a considerable quantity of a fine "Carmine red" fibrous secretion was emitted from the abdomen, and stained paper, ivory &c, of a bright colour." CD 10 March 1832, Bahia Blanca. *Beagle animal notes* (1832–33): CUL MS.DAR.29.1.A1-A49.

Blue Vapour
"The remotest discoveries of the Chemist, the Botanist, or Mineralogist, will be as proper objects of the Poet's art as any upon which it can be employed." William Wordsworth, Preface to *Lyrical Ballads* (1800).

"I a geologist…truly poetical. (V[ery] Wordsworth about sciences being sufficiently habitual to become poetical)": CD, 'M' notebook [Metaphysics on morals and speculations on expression (1838)]: CUL MS.DAR.125.

"The knowledge of…the Man of science…is personal and individual acquisition, slow to come to us…" William Wordsworth, Preface to *Lyrical Ballads*.

"I am at present red-hot with spiders": CD to John Henslow, 18 May/16 June 1832: Kew Henslow letters: 12. By kind permission of the Trustees of the Royal Botanic Gardens, Kew. John Stevens Henslow (1796–1861) was Darwin's botany professor at Cambridge and later, a mentor and good friend.

See also Randal Keynes, *Annie's Box: Charles Darwin, His Daughter and Human Evolution*, Fourth Estate, London, 2001 for more about the intersection between Charles Darwin and William Wordsworth.

How to Geologise Abroad
Darwin reportedly wrote a pamphlet later in life called: "How to Geologise Abroad".

Humboldt, Alexander von (1769–1859) and Bonpland, Aimé, *Personal narrative of travels to the equinoctial regions of the New Continent, during the years 1799–1804, with maps, plans, &c*, 7 vols, Longman, Hurst, Rees, Orme and Brown, London (1818–29). Written in French by Alexander de Humboldt, and translated into English by Helen Maria Williams.

Lapilli: 'little stones' that fall from the air during a volcanic eruption.

"Snow: Earthquakes: Thunder Storms" CD, 'Faulkland Maldonado (excursion) Rio Negro to Bahia Blanca'. *Beagle* Field Notebook: EH.1.14. The original notebook is kept at Down House, the property of English Heritage.

Rio, June, 1832
Probably a kletoparasitic species of spider—one that intrudes into the webs of larger spiders and eats their prey.

Jungle
"started about 1/2 after six. & passed over scorching plains cactuses & other succulent plants (on the decayed & stunted trees beautiful parasitic Orchis with a delicious smell) glaring hot: therm: in pocket 96°. — inland brackish lakes with numerous birds. white Egrets — Herons — whites & cormorants. lost our way", CD 9 April 1832, *Beagle* Field Notebook:

EH.1.10. The original notebook is kept at Down House, the property of English Heritage.

See also: Rio de Janeiro, May–June 1832, in Darwin, C. R., *Journal of researches into the natural history and geology of the countries visited during the voyage of H.M.S. Beagle round the world, under the Command of Capt. Fitzroy*, 2nd edition, John Murray, London, 1845.

Forms for Rapture

Darwin went to the Birmingham Music Festival in 1829 with his brother Erasmus and was greatly taken by the soprano Maria Malibran, whose voice caused his spine to go cold.

In his *Voyage of the* Beagle, Rio de Janeiro, May–June 1832, Darwin describes catching fireflies and also their luminous larvae: "When the insect was decapitated the rings remained uninterruptedly bright, but not so brilliant as before." Darwin, C. R., *Narrative of the surveying voyages of His Majesty's Ships Adventure and Beagle between the years 1826 and 1836, describing their examination of the southern shores of South America, and the Beagle's circumnavigation of the globe. Journal and Remarks* [later known as *Voyage of the Beagle*], Harry Colburn, London, 1839.

On the Subject of Untimely Extinction

Captain Fitzroy really did believe that the Mastodon became extinct because it couldn't fit into the ark.

El Naturalista

On Darwin's overland trip from 'Patogones' to Bahia Blanca in August, 1833, a band of Gauchos accompanied Darwin to Rio Colorado to meet General Juan Manuel de Rosa who would grant 'El Naturalista' permission to proceed North.

1832–1833 Maldonado: "I carried with me some promethean matches, which I ignited by biting; it was thought so wonderful that a man should strike fire with his teeth, that it was usual to collect the whole family to see it: I was once offered a dollar for a single one." Darwin, C. R., *Narrative of the surveying voyages of His Majesty's Ships Adventure and Beagle between the years 1826 and 1836... Journal and Remarks*, Henry Colburn, London, 1839.

Down the Backbone

The entire account of the *Beagle* visit to Tierra Del Fuego, including the waltzing Fuegians and the naked woman in the boat is described in Darwin's *Voyage of the Beagle*, 1839. In it, Darwin calls this part of South America 'the backbone'.

"Captain Cook has compared it to a man clearing his throat." Darwin, C. R., *Narrative of the surveying voyages of His Majesty's Ships Adventure and Beagle between the years 1826 and 1836... Journal and Remarks*, Henry Colburn, London, 1839.

"What a scale of improvement is comprehended between the faculties of a Fuegian savage & a Sir Isaac Newton—" CD, 25 February 1834, Tierra del Fuego: *Beagle* Diary (1831–36): EH: 88202366. The original is held at Down House, the property of English Heritage.

There is a complicated and terrible story about the three Fuegians: York Minister, Fuegia Basket, and Jemmy Button (exchanged for a pearl button) previously 'captured' by Captain Fitzroy, brought back to England, schooled and returned to Tierra Del Fuego with their linen, wine glasses and tea trays as 'civilisation' missionaries. On their return, York Minister married Fuegia Basket but both were robbed by the other Fuegians. York and Basket then robbed Jemmy Button and disappeared. On the *Beagle's* return, Darwin and Fitzroy found Jemmy Button had gone back to his old ways.

The Tortoise

Darwin writes in his field notebook about riding the back of the giant Galapagos' tortoises, though he claimed them difficult to balance on. 9 October 1835.

Salina: salt lake

Falls at Weatherboard, Australia, January 17th, 1836

During the *Beagle* voyage in Australia, Darwin hired a driver to take him across the Blue Mountains of New South Wales to Bathurst. On the way, he stopped at a place then known as 'Weatherboard' (now known as Wentworth Falls) and walked along the creek to the cliffs overlooking the valley and the waterfall. This walk is now called 'Darwin's Walk' and there's a plaque affixed to a rock near the falls: *"Charles Darwin passed this way"*. It's 'exceedingly well worth' a visit, as Darwin himself noted.

Handel, January 17th 1836

'Yammerschooner': Darwin reported in his *Voyage of the Beagle* that the Tierra del Fuegians yelled 'yammerschooner' whenever they wanted something from the English foreigners. Roughly translates as: 'give to me'.

"No one can stand unmoved in these solitudes without feeling that there is more in man than the mere breath of his body." And speaking of Patagonia: "Why…do these arid wastes take so firm possession of the memory?" CD September 1836 *Beagle* Diary (1831–36): EH: 88202366. The original is held at Down House, the property of English Heritage.

"we may all be netted together:": 'B' notebook [Transmutation of Species (1837–38)]: CUL MS.DAR.121. Darwin had not yet written these words when he visited Australia, nor were his ideas on the origin of species developed at that point. Though Darwin did not begin his first 'transmutation of species' notebook until 1837, he'd had 'vague doubts' on the nature of descent from about 1832, during the *Beagle* voyage, and indeed, his son Francis also believes that his thinking on evolution can be dated from 1832, but most especially after 1835, when he first visited the Galapagos Islands (See *The Foundations of the Origins of the Species*, edited by Francis Darwin, Cambridge University Press, Cambridge, 1909). I have therefore taken the poetic liberty to ascribe certain thoughts to CD during his time in Australia that might have occurred vaguely, haphazardly, but most probably did not occur concretely until a later date. I was struck looking at Wentworth Falls in the Blue Mountains, NSW (previously Weatherboard which Darwin visited during his inland trip to Bathurst) how the pattern of water falling over the rocks resembled the drawing of descent that he would later make, but at that time had not yet drawn. In doing this, I have I suppose, conceptually time-travelled, one of the blessed things about being a poet as opposed to a biographer.

"Nevertheless you have expressed my inward conviction, though far more vividly and clearly than I could have done, that the Universe is not the result of chance." CD, to W. Graham, 3 July 1881: CUL MS.DAR.144: 83, 345.

Return to Weatherboard, January 24–25th, 1836

Darwin notes the 'never failing eucalyptus' [Darwin, C. R., *Narrative of the surveying voyages of His Majesty's Ships Adventure and Beagle between the years 1826 and 1836... Journal and Remarks*, Henry Colburn London, 1839] and his stay in the little Inn at Weatherboard on Sunday 17 January, as well as his return through bush fires and subsequent day in bed at Weatherboard, on 24 and 25 January: He wrote: "Ill in bed." "Quiet, drizzly rain; all still dripping from eaves undulating woodland horizon of lost in thin mist— cold—" 'Sydney Mauritius' (January 1836) *Beagle* field notebook: EH.1.3; while the *Beagle* Diary notes: "all was still...the air was cold & comfortless". *Beagle* Diary (1831–6): EH: 88202366. These original notebooks are held at Down House, the property of English Heritage.

The Sailor

The sailors on board the *Beagle* called CD 'Philosopher' or 'Philos'.

"I hate every wave of the ocean." Darwin also speaks of how returning men of war: "light their tobacco pipes with Pound notes, to testify their joy." CD to William Darwin Fox from Hobart, 15 February 1836: CCLC Fox 48.

"I suppose I shall remain through the whole voyage, but it is a sorrowful long fraction of one's life; especially as the greatest part of the pleasure is in anticipation." CD to W.D. Fox, May 1832: CCLC Fox 46.

"like a Vulture I devoured yours & other letters". CD to W.D. Fox, 12–13 November, 1832: CCLC Fox 46a.

"As for the good sisterhood at home, they remain, in statu quo, and long may they so remain." CD to W.D. Fox, 12 March 1837: CCLC Fox 51. The letters of Charles Darwin and William Darwin Fox by kind permission of the Master and Fellows, Christ's College, Cambridge.

"A person in a hot country might with closed eyes tell what colour the ground was on which he was walking." Bahia, 29 February 1832: CUL MS.DAR.30.18-21.

'odious South America', letter from Darwin's sister to CD 22 November 22 1835: CUL MS.DAR.97 (B).

Megatherium, a huge relative of the sloth. When Darwin discovered its fossil teeth, jawbone and skull (between 22 September and early October 1832), he at first thought it was a rhinoceros.

Darwin wondered in 'M' notebook (1838): "one can dream of intense scarlet?" CUL MS.DAR.125.

– III –

"this odious dirty smokey town", CD to W.D. Fox, 12 March 1837: CCLC Fox 51. By kind permission of the Master and Fellows, Christ's College, Cambridge.

John Gould, Superintendent of Stuffed Birds
English ornithologist (1804–1881), preserver at the museum of the Zoological Society of London, he identified Darwin's 'finches' upon Darwin's return from the *Beagle* voyage.

Metaphysical Thoughts, Con't
Darwin wrote to Henslow about the bed of oyster shells he'd discovered in Chiloe, that grew a forest of trees 350 feet above sea level. March 1835.

"The free will (if so called/makes change in bodily organization of oyster. so may free will make change in man...Probably some error in argument, should be grateful if it were pointed out." 'M' notebook (1838): CUL MS.DAR.125.

The young Darwin was greatly influenced by the ideas of the geologist Charles Lyell (1797–1875), who believed that geological change was wrought slowly – not cataclysmically, or in one single upheaval – over a long span of time; it was the product of climates, volcanoes, the Earth's shifting. Darwin read volumes one and two of Lyell's *Principles of Geology* while on the *Beagle* voyage and applied Lyell's principles to the geological formations he found on his travels. He studied the high ancient shell beds; he experienced an earthquake at sea on 20 February 1835 and saw its subsequent damage on shore at Concepción. He found fresh mussel beds above the high tide line thrown up by the earthquake, proving that formations such as the Andes was sea floor that rose gradually in 'bursts' over a period of time.

London (II)

Extract from *Clarissa, or, the History of a Young Lady*, by Samuel Richardson (1748). Darwin read this book during his Christmas holidays, 1829, calling it the 'greatest novel ever written.' CD to William Darwin Fox, 3 January 1830: CCLC Fox 25. By kind permission of the Master and Fellows, Christ's College, Cambridge.

36 Great Marlborough Street

Darwin lived at this address in London after his return from the *Beagle* voyage.

Noted in 'M' notebook (1838): "3rd pleasure association: *warmth, exercise, birds singing*": CUL MS.DAR.125.

"I shall never go up in a balloon...& *"Marry, Marry, Marry"* from 'This is the Question Marry Not Marry' [Memorandum on Marriage, 1838]: CUL MS.DAR. 210.8.2 [1].

In a letter of 1836 to a friend, Darwin described bachelors as caterpillars; in another: "As for a wife, that most interesting specimen in the whole series of vertebrate animals, Providence only know whether I shall ever capture one or be able to feed her if caught." CD to C. Whitley, 8 May 1838: BL Add 41567:248-50. By kind permission of the British Library.

Though today we attribute the phrase 'survival of the fittest' to Charles Darwin, it was in fact English philosopher Herbert Spencer (1820–1903) who first coined it in his *Principles of Biology* (1864), though he did so *after* reading Darwin's *On the origin of species*. In his fifth edition of *The Origin* (1869), Darwin himself used the phrase synonymously with 'Natural Selection'.

Is This Not Our House?

Charles and Emma's first house after they were married was number 12 Upper Gower St, London. Charles wrote to Emma: "By the way, this puts me in mind to give you a scolding, for writing to me about *"your"* house: is it not our house: what is there from me, the geologist to the black sparrows in the garden which is not your own property." Also: "Fanny has just called, she has made all enquiries about the Cook, whom Sarah recommended, & has determined she is the best, & therefore has agreed to take her at 14£ 14s per year with tea & sugar." CD to Emma Wedgwood, 6 January 1839: CUL MS.DAR.210.8:11.

In the Pantry

"Burrowing mole"; "Barking Bird" with "larvae of beetles"; "Mouse, Head of Mouse"; "shells sold in the market at Buenos Ayres for spoons", etc. 'Notes made on *Beagle*, 1832–36': 'Mammalia in spirits of wine': CUL MS.DAR.29.3.

December 27th, 1839

Charles and Emma's first son William was born on 27 December 1839.

"Lat 38°S. 25´ South. Soundings 14 fathoms. Caught by hook a specimen of genus squalus: Body 'blueish grey';...Its eye was the most beautiful thing I ever saw—pupil pale 'verdegris green' but with lustre of a jewel—appearing like a Sapphire...Good specimen for dissecting..."; "I could not exactly in this specimen see the heart..." Darwin, C. R., 'Diary of observations on Zoology of the places visited during *Beagle* Voyage', 28 August 1832: CUL MS.DAR.29.1.B.

"squalled, but no tears—touching sole of foot with spill of paper...it jerked it away very suddenly, curled its toes." Darwin kept notebooks of his observations of his children, their reactions, activities and scraps of their dialogue from the time of their birth. The above was written of William Erasmus when he was one week old. Darwin, C. R., 'Notebook of Observations on the Darwin children (1839–1856)': CUL MS.DAR.210.11.37.

– IV –

"I long for tomorrow. I feel sure I shall become deeply attached to Down..." CD to Elizabeth Darwin, 16 September 1842. The original is held at Down House, the property of English Heritage.

Coralline

Darwin refers to corals in his field notes from the *Beagle* voyage as 'corallines'. His fascination with corals led him to write a book called *The Structure and Distribution of Coral Reefs*, Smith, Elder, London, 1842.

Darwin's Geology professor at Cambridge, Adam Sedgwick (1785–1873), told his students about a spring that deposited lime on twigs, inspiring Charles to throw an entire bush into the water and bring it back covered in intricate white designs. Sedgwick displayed it in the classroom.

I've no idea if Darwin read Stendhal's *De L'Amour* (1822) but Stendhal's image of the birth of love and longing is one of a crystallised branch.

Apparently wallpaper in the 19th century was made using chalk (in which the fossilised bodies of minute sea creatures were captured). See Rebecca Stott's *Darwin and the Barnacle*, Faber & Faber, London, 2003. The image of the Darwin children licking the windowpanes for sea-salt is also referenced in Stott's book.

'Thompson's phosphorescence': John Thompson's *Zoological Researches and Illustrations; Or a Natural History of Nondescript or Imperfectly Known Animals*, (1830). In it he describes phosphorescence in the sea "*of the softest and most destructible tenderness.*" Darwin had ordered a copy of this book for the *Beagle* voyage.

The Names for Things

The Darwin's didn't get a billiard table until the children were older than they are in this poem. Charles used to spread out bones and specimens over the table when he was working.

Habit

"When a muscle is moved very often the notion becomes habitual + involuntary—when a thought is thought very often it becomes habitual + involuntary, that is involuntary memory, as in sleep—"; "habit of pondering"; "I noticed this by perceiving myself skipping when wanting not to feel angry—such efforts prevent anger." 'M' notebook (1838): MS.DAR.125.

Brodie

Brodie was the Darwin's children's Scottish nurse from 1842. She had previously worked for the writer William Makepeace Thackeray. She remained in the Darwin family's service until Annie Darwin died in 1851.

Erasmus Darwin

Erasmus Darwin was CD's paternal grandfather.

Robert Hooke's *Micrographia*, published in 1665. Erasmus Darwin owned a copy and Charles had Erasmus' copy in his own library. A very beautiful and strange book of drawings from objects under a microscope. Hooke begins with the "Observations of Bodies of the: Most simple nature first and so gradually proceed to those of a more compounded one." Most hilarious was his attempt to put a piece of 'art' under the microscope. He concluded: "For the productions of Art are such rude, mis-shapen things that when viewed with a Microscope there is little else observable but their deformity." See: CUL DAR LIB Hooke (R.).

J.B. Robinet's *Philosophical Views…* was originally published in French in 1768. I have no idea if Darwin ever saw a copy, though I presume that his grandfather Erasmus did, considering his belief in the evolution of man from shells and filaments. See: Erasmus Darwin, *Zoönomia* (1794–96).

Erasmus Darwin's poem *The Botanic Garden*, 1789.

'E conchis omnia' quoted in Erasmus Darwin's biographer Desmond King-Hele's *Erasmus Darwin and The Romantic Poets*, Palgrave Macmillan, London, 1986. Erasmus painted this evolutionary (and therefore blasphemous) motto on his carriage in 1770 but was forced to paint over it again when his neighbour told him to alter it or risk losing patients.

Ink

"selection by death" in 'First Pencil Sketch of Species Theory: Written at Maer + Shrewsbury during May + June 1842': CUL MS.DAR.6:1-13. This document was later written up into a longer essay totalling 231 pages that Darwin apparently kept hidden until 1856, when he began reworking it into *On the origin of species by means of natural selection, or the preservation of favoured races in the struggle for life*, John Murray, London, 1859.

Darwin writes of catching an octopus in St Jago. "...he twisted his body with great ease between the stones only his suckers stuck very fast to them.—"; "When on land did not walk well having difficulty in carrying its head." 28 January 1832: CUL MS.DAR 30.1-4.

Marriage

Darwin spent eight years dissecting barnacles, leading his young son George to ask one of his friends: *Where does your father do his barnacles?*

Darwin refers to a specimen of barnacle he discovered on a beach in South America during the *Beagle* voyage as *Mr Arthrobalanus.*

In a letter to Joseph Hooker, CD writes: "you will perhaps wish my Barnacles & Species theory al Diabolo together. But I don't care what you say, my species theory is all gospel—" 10 May 1848: CUL MS.DAR.114:112.

Stalked barnacle (Mrs) Ilba's minute males: "& thus fixed & half embedded in the flesh of their wives they pass their whole lives & can never move again." CD to John Henslow, 1 April 1848: CUL MS.DAR.93:A17.

"At last gleams of light have come, & I am almost convinced (quite contrary to opinion I started with) that species are not (it is like confessing a murder) immutable." CD to Joseph Hooker, 11 January 1844: CUL MS.DAR.114:3.

"Man and wife being constantly together for life...": 'B' notebook (1837): CUL MS.DAR.121.

After Breakfast

"testing success of deceiving headache & found best plan was allowing my mind to skip from subject to subject as quick as it chose": 'M' notebook (1838): CUL MS.DAR.125.

Darwin was in the habit of asking himself questions in his notebooks and then later marking in the margins beside them: *"answered", "partially answered"* or *"no," "no answer."*

fixed forms eternal... as expressed in Plato's *The Republic.*

Charles and Emma were lenient, unorthodox parents. They preferred to purchase less expensive furniture and let their children have the run of the sofas, staircase (down which the children slid on a wooden board), than buy expensive things and bar the children from the parlour or the other rooms of the house, including, when deemed necessary, Charles' study.

Darwin was ironically, given the amount of dissections he had to do, overly sensitive to the sight of blood.

"everybody is insane at some time": 'M' notebook (1838): CUL MS.DAR.125.

She Played
Emma was a gifted pianist; in her youth she studied with Frédéric Chopin.

In his *Dialogues Concerning Natural Religion* (1779), David Hume joked that perhaps, instead of a creator, there was a spider: "The Brahmins assert, that the world arose from an infinite spider, who spun this whole complicated mass from his bowels..." According to his notebook of 'Books Read', Darwin was reading Hume in 1842. Darwin considered Hume—whom in his own lifetime was accused of being an atheist, though his position was actually closer to agnosticism—to be a central influence on him.

Erasmus Darwin wrote in his poem *The Botanic Garden* (1789):
"Each pendant spider winds with fingers fine
His ravel'd clue, and climbs along the line."

Definitions for Happiness
In Darwin's 'M' notebook (1838), he asked: 'What is happiness?': CUL MS.DAR.125.

Darwin kept a 'Notebook of Observations on the Darwin Children' (1839–56), which includes a lot of their dialogue and banter with their parents. As a young child, Lenny shocked himself by calling his father an 'old ass', and then confessed: "Really I didn't mean to spurt that out." CUL MS.DAR.210.11.37.

Doctor Gully's Extraordinary Water Cure Establishment
Charles and family travelled several times to Dr James Gully's spa at Malvern in the North of England for cold water cures, in order to attempt to treat Charles's incessant dyspepsia and vomiting spells, thought to be caused

by excessive mental (and perhaps, spiritual) strain. His first visit to Doctor Gully's was between March and June, 1849.

In a letter to his sister Susan, Darwin describes the rituals of rough towels, cold water scrubs and compresses that made up Dr Gully's cure: "At no time must I take any sugar, butter, spices tea bacon or anything good." CD to Susan Darwin, 19 March 1849: CUL MS.DAR.92 A7-A8.

"ah those were delightful days when one had no such organ as a stomach, only a mouth and the masticating appurtenances." CD to John Henslow, 6 May 1849: CUL MS.DAR.145:63.

The Time Traveller
An essay by Adam Gopnik beautifully suggested Darwin as a man living in two times simultaneously. Adam Gopnik, "Rewriting Nature", *The New Yorker*, 23 October, 2006.

Gaucho: nomadic 'cowboys' of the South American pampas or Patagonian grasslands.

Darwin often referred to tiny creatures and at times, his children too, as 'animalcules'.

"Marine lizard feeds on sea-weed" Darwin, C.R., *Narrative of the surveying voyages of His Majesty's Ships Adventure and Beagle between the years 1826 and 1836, describing their examination of the southern shores of South America, and the* Beagle's *circumnavigation of the globe. Journal and remarks.* Henry Colburn, London, 1839.

March, 1851
Annie Darwin was sent to Dr Gully's at Malvern in March, 1851, accompanied by her sister Henrietta and her nurse Brodie. When it appeared that Annie wouldn't recover (from what is suggested to have been tuberculosis), Darwin rushed to her side. She died in April and was buried in Malvern.

Call the Black Horses
Annie Darwin, Darwin's favourite daughter, died at Malvern on 22 April 1851. She was ten years old.

'Attach backs of Nut-hatch, flint, Hawthorn stems': Darwin carried painter Patrick Syme's *Werner's Nomenclature of Colours* (1814) on the *Beagle* voyage and used it to describe specimens by comparing them with Syme's colours of well-known objects from the Animal, Vegetable and Mineral Kingdoms. Annie also loved this poetic book. A copy is in Darwin's library (DAR LIB) now kept in the Manuscript Room at the University of Cambridge Library.

After Annie's death, Darwin stopped believing in a Christian God and in later years referred to himself as 'agnostic.'

Heaven for Women
Henrietta Darwin, apparently did indeed ask Emma, after Annie's death, where women went as the angels in the pictures were men.

$$- V -$$

"How awfully flat I should feel, if when I get my book together on species, &c &c, the whole thing explodes like an empty puff-ball." CD to Joseph Hooker, 26 March 1854: CUL MS.DAR.114:120.

In the Kitchen
Emma Darwin's recipe book is a long and fascinating list of puddings. One can't help but wonder if Darwin's indigestion was a form of lactose-intolerance further complicated by stress and metaphysical doubts: CUL MS.DAR.214.

In the Study
"Tie up the wings of large birds with string"; "To prepare the bones", etc. 'Notes made on *Beagle* 1832-6': CUL MS.DAR.29.3.

Chance & Necessity, 1858
In his book *Dear Mr Darwin: Letters on the Evolution of Life and Human Nature*, Weidenfeld & Nicolson, London, 2000, Gabriel Dover speaks of the "dual play between chance and necessity".

"The varieties of man may seem to act on each other..." Upon landing at Sydney Cove, January 12, 1836. Darwin, C. R., *Narrative of the surveying voyages of His Majesty's Ships Adventure and Beagle between the years 1826 and 1836... Journal and Remarks*, Henry Colburn, London, 1839.

In June, Charles and Emma's tenth child, Charles Waring Darwin, contracted scarlet fever. He died on 28 June 1858. He was eighteen months old.

'*On the tendencies of varieties to depart infinitely from the original type*', February 1858, Alfred Russel Wallace (1823–1913). Naturalist Wallace and Darwin had previously exchanged a few letters in which Wallace vaguely alluded to ideas that Darwin at the time didn't believe were close to his own. He encouraged Wallace to continue his work. When Wallace later sent him his paper proposing a theory akin to natural selection, Darwin was horrified. He immediately wrote to his friends Joseph Dalton Hooker (1817–1911) and Charles Lyell (1797–1875) asking advice. They arranged for a public joint presentation of Wallace and Darwin's papers on 1 July 1858, though they included unpublished work of Darwin's that established his priority.

The Stories
Emma and Charles were great readers of novels. Emma often read to Charles in the evening.

"...a pigeon has floated for 30 days in salt water with seeds in crop & they have grown splendidly & to my great surprise...I have seen dead land birds in sea-drift..." CD to Joseph Hooker, 10 December 1856: CUL MS.DAR.114:186.

Mrs. D
Mrs Grice is mentioned several times in Emma Darwin's recipe book. You can just hear her voice in the recipes she gives Emma to copy: "*Everything depends on the yeast being good.*" CUL MS.DAR.214.

Symptoms, Cures
After returning from the *Beagle* voyage, Darwin spent most of his adult life suffering from severe bouts of recurring illness. He tried almost every cure and saw many doctors, but remained undiagnosed. He had some luck with

Dr Gully at Malvern, but after Annie's death, he sought a new hydrotherapist. He began to see Dr Edward Lane, who ran a clinic, Moor Park, in Surrey, not far from Darwin's home. Dr Lane said he'd never seen a patient in so much pain as when Darwin first presented himself. In the end, Darwin preferred Dr Lane's treatment, as he didn't follow the alternative practices of Dr Gully, such as homeopathy and clairvoyance.

"but as the Spaniard says 'no hay remedio.'" CD to Catherine Darwin, 3 June 1836: CUL MS.DAR.223: 35.

The Slave
In his *Autobiography*, Darwin claimed his illness was brought on by 'excitement', though he also wrote that the 'excitement' of scientific work made him forget about, or drove away his 'daily discomfort'. He was extremely susceptible to stress. It has been suggested that Darwin suffered from panic disorder, along with many other possible diseases, both physiological and psychological, but nobody knows for sure the cause of his illnesses. I personally favour a diagnosis of existential stress combined with lactose-intolerance, despite the necessarily contentious nature of any existential claims.

Gorilla
Richard Owen (1804–1892), Royal College of Surgeons, London, the expert ape dissector, disagreed with Darwin and his theory of evolution, saying that the unique gorilla brain was so different from Man's, that Man could not have evolved from it. The gorilla had only been discovered in 1847.

'*Gorilla Quadrille For Piano flew off the shelves*': See Paul Collins, 'Histories: Gorillas, I presume', *New Scientist Magazine*, October, 2005.

Gorilla gorilla gorilla is the name given to the sub-species Western Lowland Gorilla. It was actually the American Reverend Thomas Savage who first coined the name *gorilla* for the skulls of the apes he found.

George Wombwell showed exotic animals in Soho. He began to tour the fairs of Britain in 1810, calling himself Wombwell's Travelling Menagerie. The gorilla in the poem was exhibited by Wombwell's in the late 1850's and is reported to have died of pneumonia in 1856. Some sources refer to it as the first live gorilla to leave Africa (and be displayed in England) and that people flocked to see it; others state that Wombwell's believed they had a chimpanzee, not a gorilla, and that it wasn't until the gorilla's death that they realised it was in fact a juvenile gorilla. These sources also claim that the 'chimp' was called Jenny and wore clothes but perhaps there is some confusion here with the orangutan Jenny of the 1830's that Darwin saw in the Zoological Society Gardens.

The eccentric and taxidermist Charles Waterton liked to create stuffed 'creature' sculptures by sewing together parts of different animals.

The Orchis Bank

"There is grandeur in this view of life, with its several powers, having been originally breathed into a few forms or into one..." Charles Darwin, *On the origin of species by means of natural selection...*, 1st edition, John Murray, London, 1859.

"There is a grandeur in this view of life, with its several powers, having been originally breathed by the Creator into a few forms or into one..." Charles Darwin, *On the origin of species by means of natural selection...*, 2nd edition, John Murray, London, 1860.

"from so simple a beginning..." ibid

"endless forms most beautiful and most wonderful..." ibid.

Darwin describes seeing the lightning bolts in Maldonado (May 1833). Darwin, C.R., *Narrative of the surveying voyages of His Majesty's Ships Adventure and Beagle between the years 1826 and 1836, describing their examination of the southern shores of South America, and the Beagle's circumnavigation of the globe. Journal and remarks.* 1832–1836, Henry Colburn, London, 1839.

In Charles's sketch of Annie after her death: "[Annie] liked to name the precise colours of things she found—matching objects to colour samples." CD, 'Our poor child, Annie' [Darwin's reminiscence of Anne Elizabeth Darwin (30 April 1851)]: CUL MS.DAR.210.13.40.

Darwin's daughter Henrietta claimed that her father never again spoke of Annie after her death.

"I am a withered leaf for every subject except Science." CD to Joseph Hooker, 17 June 1868: CUL MS.DAR.94:72-3.

August 3, 1868
In the summer of 1868, the Darwins' rented a cottage from the photographer Julia Margaret Cameron and she took Charles's portrait.

Lesson
Ourang-Outang is the way Darwin spelled what we now know as 'Orangutan' after visiting one at the Zoological Society in March 1838. He wrote about the visit in a letter home on 1 April 1838.

Sir John Herschel wrote "Time! Time! Time!" to geologist Charles Lyell on 20 February 1836. He believed the Old Testament chronology was far too short to be true. Lyell was by this time a friend of Darwin's (Darwin had also met Herschel on his *Beagle* voyage), and Darwin quotes Lyell's letter in one of his own to his sister Caroline.

Repeat Lesson
After he published *The Descent of Man* in 1871, *Le Figaro* and *Punch*, among others, published cartoons of Darwin as a monkey-man. "A venerable ourang-outang, a contribution to unnatural history" (cartoon), 22 March 1871. *The Hornet*, Anon.: CUL MS.DAR.141.6.

A family attempts to rouse the worms
Darwin and his family conducted such worm experiments as he wrote *The Formation of Vegetable Mould, though the Action of Worms, with Observations on Their Habits*. John Murray, London, 1881.

The Movements and Habits of Truth
Darwin published an article called 'On the Movements and Habits of Climbing Plants' in 1865. He later expanded it into a book of the same name, published by John Murray, London, 1875.

The Death of the Transmutationist

Darwin did have a dream—around the time he was realising the truth of his species theory, that is, the transmutation of species—of a man being hung.

"Animals with affections, imitation, fear. pain, sorrow for the dead." 'B' notebook (1837): CUL MS.DAR.121.

– VII –

"Fear must be simple instinctive feeling: I have awakened in the night being slightly unwell & felt so much afraid." 'M' notebook (1838): CUL MS.DAR.125.

The Last Notebook

"*Do monkeys cry? (They whine like children)*": 'M' notebook (1838): CUL MS.DAR.125.

The Green Need, April, 1882

"why is life short—' 'B' notebook (1837): CUL MS.DAR.121.

In a letter to Charles Lyell, Sir John Hershel wrote that the 'mystery of mysteries'—was how new species appear on Earth. For Darwin, who quoted this letter in one of his own to his sister, the mystery to solve was also how species disappear. Indeed, he quoted this in his introduction to the first edition of *On the origin of species*.

Darwin claimed he was agnostic, but believed that natural laws, rather than the will of a God, was in charge of this world and he said little of the next, referring instead to "conflicting vague probabilities." Some call Darwin a Stoic, but he was not indifferent to grief and pain; in fact, just the opposite.

Darwin wrote: "Montaigne—He will observe one does not fear death from its pain but one only fears that pain which is connected with death!" 'M' notebook (1838): CUL MS.DAR.125.

Afterwards

When I visited Down House, the curator showed me some of Emma's personal things, one of which was her absolutely tiny gold wedding band.

Emma

Laura Forster, E.M. Forster's aunt stayed with the Darwins in 1882. She reported that Darwin came into the drawing room and said: "The clocks go so dreadfully slowly, I have come in here to see if this one gets over the hours any quicker than the study one does." Randal Keynes, *Annie's Box: Charles Darwin, His Daughter and Human Evolution*, Fourth Estate, London, 2001.

Again, Darwin never stated himself to be an atheist, but rather an agnostic. His doubts about God, religion and faith became a matter of continual questioning, a lifelong investigation.

"If I had to live my life again…" quoted by Francis, Darwin, ed., *The life and letters of Charles Darwin, including an autobiographical chapter, vol. 1.*, John Murray, London, 1887.

Acknowledgements

I am very grateful to the Australia Council for the Arts' Literature Board for awarding me a residency during the summer of 2007 at the Tyrone Guthrie Centre in Annaghmakerrig, County Monaghan, Ireland, where I wrote this book.

My greatest thanks to Judith Beveridge for her support, insight, kindness and great care with this manuscript.

For help and encouragement during the research and long gestation of this project I'd like to thank:
Adam Perkins, Curator of Scientific Manuscripts, The Darwin Archive, Cambridge University Library, Cambridge
Dr Pat Donlon and the Tyrone Guthrie Centre, County Monaghan, Ireland
Dr Ian Henderson, The Menzies Centre for Australian Studies, King's College, London
Sam Kuper, Darwin Correspondence Project, Cambridge
English Heritage, Down House, Kent
Candace Guite and the staff of Christ's College Old Library, Cambridge
Dr Elinor Shaffer, FBA, University of London
Ivor Indyk
Peter Bishop, Varuna Writers' Centre, Katoomba, NSW
Terri-ann White, Kate McLeod, Jade Knight and everybody at UWA Press.
Keith Feltham
Benython Oldfield
The Cameron Creswell Agency, Sydney
Lucy Luck and the Lucy Luck Agency, London
Dame Gillian Beer
Bob Bloomfield, Katie Edwards and those working on Darwin200 from the Natural History Museum, London <www.darwin200.org>, a programme celebrating Charles Darwin's life, his ideas and their impact around his two-hundredth anniversary.

For providing me with second homes as well as great support and friendship while constantly en route: Cindy Ryan, Genevieve Maynard, Sarah Ducker & Co and Kathleen Farrar.

To my father, who first sat me on his knee and explained evolution to me.

And finally, but mostly, to Ewan Morrison for his unwavering belief in me and his huge brain; a true Darwinian.

EMILY BALLOU is a poet, screenwriter and novelist. She was the winner of The Judith Wright Prize for Poetry and her poems have been published internationally for nineteen years. Her novels *Father Lands* and *Aphelion* were both published by Picador. *The Darwin Poems* were written on an Australia Council for the Arts residency in County Monaghan, Ireland. It is her first collection of poetry.

Printed in the United Kingdom by
Lightning Source UK Ltd., Milton Keynes
141307UK00001B/13/P